BAIL OUT over the BALKANS

ESCAPE THROUGH NAZI-OCCUPIED YUGOSLAVIA

by
RICHARD MUNSEN

•

with
KATHERINE MUNSEN

Bail Out over the Balkans

ISBN: 9781731363855

Cover Artwork Provided by
Rod Bohner

Graphic Designers
Molly Halstead
Mardell Christian

Editors
Virginia Harding Roth
Diana Swanson
Paul Munsen

www.munsen.com

This book is dedicated to those courageous Partisans and their followers who made countless sacrifices to save us from capture — even death.

FOREWORD

While sitting around the fireplace in a cabin at Estes Park on a cold June evening in 1982, Bob Brown and my husband, Dick, started reminiscing about World War II and their trek through Yugoslavia nearly forty years before. Charlotte, Bob's wife, and I were fascinated. Most of these stories we had never heard. In the years immediately after the war, the men's experiences as "evadees" had been too traumatic and painful to discuss and relive.

In the winter and spring of 1944 Dick was a B-17 pilot flying out of Amendola, Italy. Assigned to the 414th Squadron of the 97th Bomb Group, Dick had flown 22 missions.

1st Lt. Richard Munsen, Age 22

i

Bob, a waist gunner with the 463rd Bomb Group, had arrived at Amendola on March 14th. Losses of planes and men had been heavy the winter of '44 and replacement crews arrived each week.

Sgt. Robert Brown, Age 20

On March 18th the 97th Bomb Group was scheduled to bomb the airdrome at Udine in Northern Italy. Because German resistance was expected to be light, the mission was dubbed a "milk run," and regarded as a good time for men from new crews to be interspersed with more experienced crews. Bob, navigator William Seward, and bombardier Thomas Howard replaced Dick's regular crew members, Calvin Churchill, Harold Shapiro, and Sanford Plautz. Bob was flying his first mission. As he told us, Dick was to teach him the ropes, but no one told him those ropes would be attached to a parachute.

Flying Fortresses and Liberators, about 350 altogether, took part in that air raid. Dick's squadron was the last element in the last group, a touchy spot to be.

B-17s flying in formation – tail markings identify the 414th squadron

About thirty minutes from the target eight German fighters attacked bombers on the outer edge of the formation, fatally damaging three planes in the 414th squadron. Dick's was one of them. The crew bailed out, landing in German occupied territory.

Conversation around that Estes Park fireplace turned to incidents still vivid in our husbands' minds... the day they hid in a cellar while the house was searched by Germans... the time they were waiting in a church and a German Stuka strafed the town... the night the dog barked, warning the Germans and preventing the men from escaping to Italy. These were traumatic events and they needed to be written down and saved for the children and grandchildren.

I picked up a pencil and a yellow pad of paper and started taking notes.

When we returned from our vacation, Dick began checking on other members of his crew. The Midwesterners, tail gunner Vern Curry, ball turret gunner Cletus Reiss, Dick, and Bob had several reunions in the years that followed. Copilot Irv Williamson joined the group for the June 1990 reunion.

Curry, Reiss, Matusic, Brown, and Munsen met in September 1993

As the men recalled incidents from their 45 days as evadees in Yugoslavia, I took notes and taped their conversations. Forty-five years takes its toll. Names, places and dates had faded, but Bob Brown had an ace in the hole — a diary. He had carried a small notebook in his button-down shirt pocket, jotting down a few lines each day about important events. He hadn't known the names of all the towns visited, but when he heard a name, he wrote it down, often phonetically.

Airmen had been warned not to keep a diary in occupied countries in case the notes would fall into the hands of the Germans, implicating the people in the resistance movement. Bob had identified towns where people had provided the men with food and shelter and had written about major incidents. He justified keeping the diary because of its small size. He claimed if he had been captured, he could have eaten the few pages containing information relevant to the Germans.

Bob's diary provided invaluable information for reconstructing the long trek through Yugoslavia.

Sample pages from Bob Brown's diary written in Yugoslavia 1944

With the diary and a 1944 Air Force topographical map, we could trace the men's route through Slovenia, Croatia and Bosnia. It was frustrating not to be able to identify the first two towns where the men had been in hiding. Either they were too small to find on a map or the spelling was incorrect. Also, his diary ended when the men reached the airstrip north of Tito's headquarters and no one knew exactly how many days they had waited for a plane to fly them to Italy.

I started writing letters to the Veteran's Administration, to the Department of the Air Force, the State Department, the National Archives, and the Imperial War Museum in London. The crew had met Allied liaison officers from Britain and the U.S. Surely their reports would provide information about assistance given downed Allied airmen by the Partisans, followers of Tito, leader of the Yugoslav Communist Party.

We visited the library located at the Air Force Base at Maxwell Field, Alabama, and found reports of the 414th squadron and 97th Bomb Group during the two months Dick was flying from Amendola. Information included data on missions, but there were no reports from U.S. liaison serving in Yugoslavia.

The most important information gained from Air Force records was in escape statements given by Dick's crew upon their return to Bari, Italy on May 2. Included were names of some towns visited, encounters with the enemy and the date when the men were flown out of Yugoslavia. Now more towns could be added to the men's route and the date when they arrived in Italy could be fixed. But to write a story about the men's experiences, more detail was needed.

Hoping Yugoslavia would have some records about Partisan assistance given our airmen, I wrote to the University of Ljubljana in Slovenia. I received a cordial reply written in German from Dr. Tone Ferenc, history professor at the university. He enclosed copies of pages from a 1946 publication "Allied Airmen and Prisoners of War rescued by the Slovene Partisans." The names, dates of landing in Yugoslavia, and serial numbers of Dick's crew were listed along with those of many other Allied airmen. Now I was making progress.

Through the Veteran's Administration I wrote to all the men who had parachuted into Yugoslavia on March 18. I received letters from four: Edward Adams, Edward Doran, Sam Schnear and Elbert Kuch. They were flying tail-end Charlie and were shot down just before Dick's plane was attacked. They described their parachute jump and isolated incidents and impressions.

Then, one Sunday morning in early February 1990, we received a telephone call that made it possible to write this story. The caller was a man named Bailey Gordon, the copilot on Edward Adams' plane. Bailey remembered Dick and had, indeed, walked out of Yugoslavia with him. When Bailey was granted leave to go home to Dallas in mid-May 1944, he knew his adventures as an evadee would make a great story. A friend, who planned to write the book, filled 23 pages of typed notes as Bailey recounted his experiences. The woman moved to California, taking the notes with her, but as the years passed, they remained untouched and the book was never written.

Forty years later the typewritten notes were returned to Bailey. They seemed to have been saved for a purpose. When Bailey sent the packet to me, I felt duty-bound to carry through with the project.

Day before we left, (2) we saw German planes in sky. Big air battle. With B'17's and B'24's from Italian base.

Back to Del Nitche. People fed them. Boiled potatoes. Gave each one four. Saved them because they would be hungrier later. Left here about 8:30 or 9:30 that night. Walked till 4:30 or 6:00 the next morning. Hurry to get to town. Got get and have to leave again. Back to Marcopol.

Got a piece of sausage and bread. Did not let us leave. Tried to get Part. Commandant to let themgo back to Del Nice. But they had others there now to care for. Stayed here about 4 days thinking every day that they would leave. Wanted to make it anyway.

Got hair cut and shave. About 2nd in all this time. Made up a list of supplies to send through to American headquarters. So that Americans could drop them to the boys.

4th day----Heard that Del Nice had been bombed by the Germans. Dropping leaflets telling them that they were going to bomb every town on the map. Bombers came over at about 1000 feet. We thought they were reconissance. He leveled offand flew straight line down middle of town, dropping four bombs immediately above heads of BG and another boy. He shouted, erratically, "My God, they're bombing us!"

Sample page from Bailey Gordon's account dictated in May 1944

Writing this book has been like working on a giant jigsaw puzzle. Bob's diary written on the scene, escape statements given by the men on May 2, conversations from crew members, and the unique authentic details contained in Bailey's account formed the foundation. When possible, dialogue was taken from taped conversations.

Political and military conditions in Croatia in spring of 1944 are available in books written by Allied liaison officers working with Tito's Partisans. Surprisingly, most of the authors did not mention the protection given Allied airmen by the Partisans. Many pieces of the puzzle have been lost, but those parts remaining provide a good picture of the struggles the men faced, and the unusual sacrifices made by the Partisans.

Before missions, the men were briefed on procedures for bailing out should the occasion arise. Informed about two organized underground units in Yugoslavia, they were told how the groups could be identified. They were warned about the Ustashi, Croats who had collaborated with the Germans, but they knew little about the political situation in the country.

After the Germans invaded Yugoslavia in April 1941, two puppet states were created: Croatia and Serbia. The Germans handed Croatia over to the Fascist Ustashi and its leader, Ante Pavelic, who assumed the title of Chief of State. The fanatical Ustashi "cleansed" the new state by exterminating Jews, Communists, Muslims and Greek Orthodox Serbs. Not even the Nazis exceeded their ferocity. The smaller Serbian puppet state was under command of General Milan Nedic.

While some of the people collaborated with the Germans, many others joined resistance groups. Two main groups emerged: Chetniks under Mihailovich, a Serb and former General of the Yugoslav Army, and the Yugoslav Communist Party, better known as the Partisans, under the leadership of Tito.

Differences in aims between the two groups led to differences in tactics. When the Chetnik resistance led to reprisals by the Germans, Mihailovich decided they should conserve their strength and wait for an Allied invasion. Since Mihailovich was convinced the Axis would eventually lose the war, he decided his most dangerous enemy was Tito and the Partisans. Consequently, the Chetniks greatly reduced their activity against Germany and concentrated on the Partisans.

The political situation in Yugoslavia was enormously complex, marked by religious passions and deeply rooted ethnic divisions. Tito, however, was not identified with any single nationality. He appealed to all groups who had a burning desire for freedom and wanted better economic conditions.

After the German invasion in 1941, King Peter and his government were exiled in England. Britain recognized the Chetniks, who represented the old Royal Yugoslav government, and sent them liaison officers, guns, ammunition and other supplies. Eager to find out who was really fighting the Germans, the British sent Major William Jones to Slovenia in May 1943. The first representative of the British Intelligence Service to be affiliated with Tito's Partisans, Major Jones was to obtain information about Partisan movements, their positions, and find out how effective they were in fighting the Germans. Brigadier Fitzroy Maclean, Captain F. W. Deakin, Major Eden, Randolph Churchill, Colonel Moore, Major Lynn Farish, and others followed.

Maclean was recalled to North Africa at the time of the Teheran Conference in December 1943. He reported that because of Partisan resistance, the Germans had more troops than ever before in Yugoslavia — 200,000 of their own soldiers and 160,000 Bulgarian and quisling Serb and Croat forces. These were men Hitler sorely needed on other fronts.

In spring of 1944, Tito's army numbered about 290,000 men and women. He had the manpower to fight the Germans but needed weapons, food, equipment, air support and medical aid. After Maclean's visit, the British realized that Tito was far more useful to the Allies than Mihailovich. Beginning in January 1944 the Partisans were to receive Allied support rather than the Chetniks.

By March of 1944, arms and supplies were arriving regularly by boat or dropped via parachutes to the Partisans. British and U.S. officers who parachuted into Yugoslavia were attached to Partisan units and under the general command of Tito and his commanders.

Many of the Yugoslavs recognized Allied bombers as theirs. When they saw parachutes in the sky, they scoured the countryside to find and protect the airmen who were helping the Partisan cause by bombing the Germans. The underground assisting downed Allied airmen was well established by the time Dick and his crew parachuted into Croatia.

One of the men helped by Tito's Partisans in the spring of 1944 should have written this book. None of Dick's crew nor Bailey Gordon could be persuaded to tackle the project. As Dick said, "I don't need to write the story, I lived it."

After transcribing tapes of the men's conversations, reading Bailey's account and seeing Bob's diary, I had to tell their story. It could not die with the men. Our children were clamoring for the book, so I chose to write it for them and the children of the other crew members. They deserve to know the dangers their fathers and grandfathers experienced and the courage with which they faced difficult situations.

Dick has written the mayors of several towns in Croatia, expressing appreciation for the protection and kindnesses extended him in the spring of 1944. Saying "thank you" in person was long overdue. With another civil war raging in Bosnia, a visit to the old "Yugoslavia" seemed inadvisable. But miracles still happen. Ivo Matusic, a Partisan leader in the Kastav area where Dick and most of his crew landed, flew from his home in Matulji, Croatia, in May 1993, to St. Louis where he attended the convention of the Air Forces Escape and Evasion Society. In his address at the AFEES meeting Ivo stated:

"Hundreds of American airmen were forced to land in our territory. During those hard times, when the black cloud of Nazism hung over Europe, when food was scarce, we gladly shared what we had with our American allies.

Events we faced during the Second World War happened behind major front lines. But for us Croats and our neighbors, the Slovenes, it was the battleground where we fought to help and save our allies in distress. Humanity, sincerity and openness helped our friendship last to this day.

Our great wish is to keep the memory of the happenings during the Second World War alive, the fight for freedom from Nazi tyranny. Your planes were symbols of freedom to us. Experiences like this need to be transferred to our grandchildren, with the hope they will know how to keep these ties and ideals alive."

Dick and I met Ivo in St. Louis and brought him to our home for a week. With the help of an interpreter more pieces were added to the story, including Partisan activities and the names of the first two towns that offered the men shelter and protection.

Ivo Matusic, left, visits with Dick in May 1993
(Photo by Doug Smith, The Daily Tribune)

After seeing first-hand the sacrifices the Partisans and their followers made for a cause they hoped would bring them freedom from poverty and freedom to make choices, it has been tragic to see the people in the Balkans devastated by another war. Whether we are Croats, Serbs, Bosnians or Americans, we share the same desire for independence.

While writing the story I received encouragement from five writers I met at Iowa City Elderhostel and the members of the Northcrest Writing Group in Ames, Iowa. I am grateful to Hazel Lipa, leader of Northcrest Mailers who helped refine the text, and to Virginia Harding Roth and Diana Swanson who served as editors.

Our children requested this book be written in the first person. Since I am married to the pilot, and he and three members of the crew have regularly checked the manuscript, it is merely my pen that tells their story.

Katherine Munsen

AUTHOR'S INTRODUCTION

On December 7, 1943, my B-17 crew and I took off from Morrison Field, West Palm Beach, Florida, with Italy as our final destination.

Original Crew – Names Left to Right
Front: Richard Munsen, Irv Williamson, Harold Shapiro, Sanford Plauz
Back: Harley Spoon, Paul Marion, Calvin Churchill, Cletus Reiss, Cecil Sullivant, Vern Curry

Three months earlier, on September 9, the Allied Fifth Army had landed at Salerno. They encountered heavy resistance. As the troops moved slowly inland the Germans retreated to a position north of Naples, building fortifications across the boot of Italy that became known as the Gustav Line.

The Allies had hoped to be in Rome by Christmas, but the snow-choked roads and rough terrain favored the enemy. Weeks of rain and snow created a quagmire and greatly handicapped the movement of men and heavily mechanized equipment.

My crew and I landed at Casablanca on December 18. We were delayed in North Africa 32 days waiting for repairs on our plane.

Camels pulling a wooden plow near a hut in Dakar, West French Africa

When we finally joined the 414th squadron in southern Italy on January 22, the Fifth Army was still mired in mud, struggling to dislodge the Germans from the Gustav Line.

January 22 marked the infamous landing of two divisions of VI Corps at Anzio, sixty miles north of German fortifications. They encountered little initial resistance, but while waiting for reinforcements our troops were counter-attacked and surrounded by the Germans. Even with air and sea support VI Corps remained trapped on the beachhead for four months.

The Fifteenth Air Force, based on airfields near Foggia, was established to bomb targets in Germany and its satellites. With the Fifth Army stagnated in southern Italy, the ground troops needed all the air support they could get. The main mission for the medium bombers and fighters in the Twelfth Air Force was to support ground troops, but the B-17s and B-24s in the Fifteenth were often called upon to assist.

Our plane was one of about 300 heavies that bombed German troop concentrations near Anzio on two occasions. When the target was marshalling yards, railroad communications were severed, forcing the enemy to move ammunition and supplies by trucks more than a hundred miles at night to their troops defending the Gustav Line.

The decision to bomb Monte Cassino was devised to support the ground troops. This historic monastery was reduced to a pile of rubble by our B-17s on February 15th and the Germans, who had not formerly used the shrine for defense, moved in and set up their artillery. The enemy position was more impregnable than before. All winter and spring the Fifth Army was stalemated north of Naples and VI Corps was trapped on the beach at Anzio.

While the infantry and support troops were trying to crack German defenses on the ground, we were fighting our battles in the sky. My crew flew twenty-two missions, bombing targets in Italy, France, Bulgaria and Germany.

During the "Big Week" in February, the Eighth and Fifteenth Air Forces coordinated missions, hitting the German aircraft industry for six consecutive days, February 20 - 25. My crew bombed the Messerschmitt component plant at Regensburg-Prufening on the 22nd and the Messerschmitt factory at Steyr Daimler on the 24th. We encountered layers of flak, swarms of fighters, and long-range rockets fired from twin-engine aircraft. Of the 87 bombers sent to Steyr on the 24th, seventeen were shot down by the Germans. Total Fifteenth Air Force bomber losses for the "Big Week" were 89, or 18%. Eight hundred and ninety men killed or missing. We began to wonder when our number would come up.

Ground troops could retreat when fighting a losing battle, but when a plane is fatally damaged, the only retreat is a parachute. On March 18 we had to use that parachute. For forty-five days we walked in the mountains of Yugoslavia.

This is the story I tell here.

CREW MEMBERS IN AIRCRAFT #472
414 SQUADRON – 97th BOMB GROUP

Pilot: 1st Lt. Richard Munsen, Age 22

Born in Story City IA, Dick attended Iowa State College two years before enlisting in the Army Air Force. One year after making his first flight as a cadet he flew across the Atlantic to join the 97th Bomb Group in Italy. Proud of his crew, he took his responsibilities as pilot seriously.

Copilot: 2nd Lt. Irvin Williamson, Age 25

Born and raised in Michigan, Irv joined the crew in Alexandria LA. A good photographer, he took his camera on every mission and provided many of the photos for this book.

Engineer: S/Sgt. Harley Spoon, Age 26

Spoon was a hell-raising redheaded Texan who spoke with a drawl well sprinkled with expletives. A competent and dependable flight engineer, he was a career Army Air Force man who worked hard and played hard.

Right Waist Gunner: Sgt. Robert Brown, Age 20

Bob grew up in Rennselaer IN and enlisted in the Army Air Force March 1943. He arrived in Italy on March 14, 1944, and bailed out over the Balkans on his first mission. Genial and outgoing, he recorded names of towns and main events in a diary while walking in Yugoslavia.

Ball Turret Gunner: Sgt. Cletus Reiss, Age 20

A star football player on the Assumption IL High School team, Cletus was a big fellow to ride in a ball turret. He enlisted in the Army Air Force on January 8, 1943, went to Gunnery School and joined Dick's crew at Pyote TX. Eleven months after enlisting he was on his way overseas.

Tail Gunner: Sgt. Vern Curry, Age 22

After attending Muscatine IA High School, Vern worked at the Rock Island IL Arsenal. He enlisted in the Air Force in October 1942. Trained as a mechanic, Vern volunteered for gunner training, so he could see action overseas.

Radio Operator: Sgt. Paul Marion, Age 20

After graduating from High School in Archbald, PA, Paul enlisted and was sent to Air Force Technical School. He was the first man to bail out of the crippled plane. Hiding in the mountains he was spotted by non-Partisan soldiers and turned over to the Germans and spent 13 months in a POW camp.

Left Waist Gunner: Sgt. Cecil Sullivant, Age 33

Sully was living in Memphis, TN when the draft caught him. The "old man" of the group, he was often referred to as "Pop." Short and slim, Sully fit well in the corridor of the B-17 waist. A "pack-a-day" man, Pop's first act after a mission was to light a cigarette.

CREW MEMBERS IN AIRCRAFT #644
414 SQUADRON – 97ᵗʰ BOMB GROUP

Copilot: 2nd Lt. L. Bailey Gordon, Age 21

A native of Dallas TX Bailey joined the Tactical Reconnaissance squadron in North Africa in 1943, flying P-39s and P-38s. Ordered to Italy, Bailey was transferred to B-17s. After ten hours of training he flew as copilot where needed. His detailed notes of the 45 days with the Partisans provided background for this story.

Tail Gunner: Sgt. Elbert Kuch, Age 23

Al grew up in the Los Angeles area. He enlisted in the Army Air Force in 1942 and left for overseas November 1943. Flying his 45th mission with the 414th squadron on March 18, Al was injured in his right arm and foot by rocket fire from a Focke-Wulf 190. He was in Partisan hospitals for about six months.

When new crews arrived at the airfield at Amendola, the men were separated and flew their first couple of missions with an experienced crew. By March 18, Dick and most of his crew had flown twenty or more missions. On the mission to Udine, Italy, Dick's Navigator, 2nd Lt. Harold Shapiro and his Bombardier, 2nd Lt. Sanford Plautz, and Waist Gunner Sgt. Calvin Churchill were replaced by 2nd Lt. William Seward, 2nd Lt. Thomas Howard and Sgt. Robert Brown. Lt. Howard fractured his ankle upon landing. Lt. Seward walked out with the crew.

First Lt. Edward Adams was flying his 48th mission in ship #644. Lt. Edward Doran and Sgt. Al Kuch were regular members of Adams' crew. Lt. Bailey Gordon was flying his first mission with Lt. Adams.

Richard Munsen's Original B-17 Crew
Front, left to right: Churchill, Marion, Spoon, Reiss, Curry, Sullivant
Back, left to right: Munsen, Williamson, Shapiro, Plautz

The enlisted men in Amendola, Italy – Winter 1944
Standing: Cecil Sullivant, Paul Marion, Harley Spoon, Calvin Churchill
Kneeling: Cletus Reiss, Vern Curry

Ready for Combat
Sanford Plautz, Harold Shapiro, Richard Munsen

Cleaning .50 Caliber Guns
Munsen, Curry, Sullivant, Churchill, unknown

Amendola, Italy 1944
Richard Munsen outside officer's quarters

Adjusting the Ball Turret
Cletus Reiss

Maintenance crew loading bombs into a B-17

Richard Munsen
Oxygen masks were worn above 9000 feet

Dick wearing his sheepskin flight jacket

Munsen's Yugoslav Short Snorter signed by the original crew
A short snorter is a banknote signed by people traveling together on an aircraft, a tradition
started by the Alaskan Bush flyers in the 1920s. Short snorters were signed by flight crews
during World War II and conveyed good luck to soldiers crossing the Atlantic.

Area of the U.S. Fifteenth Air Force Operations 1944

The shaded area is enlarged on the next pages and shows the route followed by Dick Munsen's crew from March 18 (Day 1) through May 1 (Day 45) 1944.

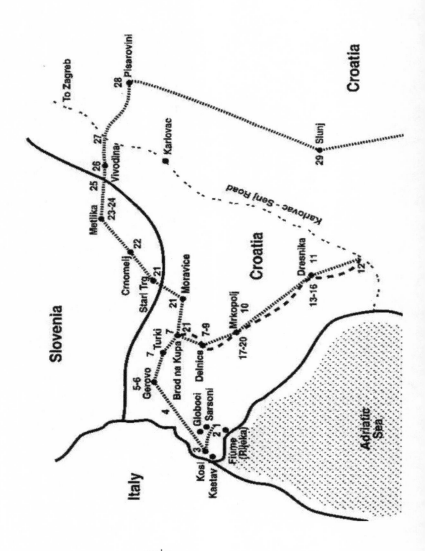

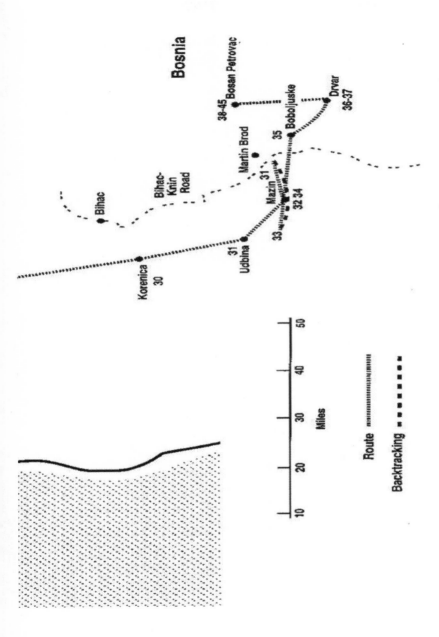

DAY ONE • SATURDAY • MARCH 18

Master and Maker, God of right
The soldier dead are at Thy gate;
Who kept the spears of honor bright
And freedom's house inviolate.

Drinkwater

We entered the briefing room. Would it be Ploesti today? Rumors were thick that we would soon be bombing the oil fields in Rumania. Today, March 18, would be my 23rd mission. Only two more to go before R&R. As I waited for the briefing officers to arrive, I recalled Homer and Coupak who had gone down with their crews a couple of weeks ago. Two planes, twenty men. The irrational reality of war always seemed most intense before the mission.

It's strange. When I thought back to the day I enlisted, September 5, 1942, I had no fear of failure or death — only the glorious expectation of becoming a pilot in the Army Air Force and flying off "into the wild blue yonder." I had said my last good-byes to my girlfriend, Kay, and my family at the Ames, Iowa railroad station. With two years of college and 46 hours of flying a little Luscombe 8A under my belt, I was ready to soar high into the clouds. One training period followed another and even though there were accidents and deaths, somehow, I never thought it would happen to me. In fact, when we were learning to fly, we were so far removed from the atrocities of war we often forgot the purpose of our training — to bomb railroad yards, ball bearing factories, and airdromes.

Now I was in Italy and the war was real. Each day's diary entry started with the number of missions completed. As I checked them off in my book, I hoped I could beat the stats and make it to the magic fifty.[1]

Out of the corner of my eye I saw the briefing officers enter. Everyone rose to attention. The group commander addressed us. "At ease, men. Today's target is the airdrome at Udine, Italy." There were obvious sighs of relief. We would not be crossing the Alps into Germany or bombing the oil fields at Ploesti.

The major uncovered the map and we noted the route we were to follow. Udine was the headquarters of the Luftwaffe in the southern theater; on the outskirts of the city was a major German airdrome that guarded the southeast approaches to Europe. We were to fly up the Adriatic and supposedly outwit the Germans by flying north into southern Austria. After a 180 degree sweep to the south, we were to approach the airdrome from the north.

---

[1] Crew members could return home to the U.S after flying 50 missions.

1

Squadron positions were assigned. Our squadron position was number 9 as shown below.

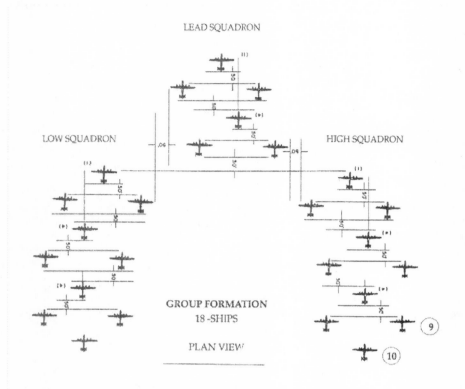

LEAD SQUADRON

LOW SQUADRON

HIGH SQUADRON

GROUP FORMATION
18 -SHIPS

PLAN VIEW

B-17 #472 was number 9 position
B-17 #644 was number 10 position

At least we wouldn't be tail-end Charlie. And there would be protection in numbers with more than 350 B-17's and B-24's hitting the area.

The major continued. "Most of your flying will be over the water. Rendezvous at 0730 hours. ETA is 1020. Reconnaissance reports flak corridor running through the target area. Cripples should try for the sea. With good fighter cover this mission should be a "milk run." The weather is expected to be in our favor. Good luck!"

The briefing was about over. We set our watches against the master chronometer. Takeoff was at 0700. We would be flying into the southern edge of the Alps — only three hours from our home base — a "milk run" the major said. But, no mission was easy. Flak was unpredictable, and those antiaircraft guns were getting more and more accurate. Heavy bombers in tight formation presented an enormous target and some were bound to be hit. And I wasn't happy with our position — number nine position of the last element in the last group — a most vulnerable spot.

As I left the briefing room, I was introduced to Lieutenants Howard and Seward, bombardier and navigator, and Brown, waist gunner for today's mission.

Three of my crew, Shapiro, Plautz, and Churchill, had been replaced by men from crews who had arrived at Amendola only two days ago. It was policy for new arrivals to fly with experienced crews the first mission or two.

Williamson and I were explaining the mission routine to Howard and Seward as we walked to the supply room to pick up our gear.

A truck took us to the flight line where I saw our ship, #472, waiting to take us to do our day's work. While I was conducting the pre-flight check with flight engineer Spoon, the crew chief greeted me. "I hear you guys are going to knock out Udine today. I hope you surprise 'em. I don't want any more holes in this airplane."

As I was preparing to climb into our plane, a sergeant came running out in the runway. Because silver bars were not available, he handed me some white tape to cover my gold ones. I had been promoted to a First Louie!

The situation had been quite different when I received my Second Louie bars. That was nine months ago in Blytheville, Arkansas. The afternoon before graduation I had a final cross-country flight to make. Coming in after dark I landed with ease and taxied down the runway. When I neared the end and applied more power to make a turn, the right wing dropped, and I began to spin around like a top. Fire engines and an ambulance came screaming toward me. Watching my dilemma were three officers and the colonel standing in the tower. My heart sank. Mother had arrived by train from Iowa for the graduation ceremony and now, at the last minute, I botched it.

The colonel stepped down from the tower and escorted me back to the flight line. We climbed into another AT-9 for a check ride. With the colonel in the right seat I shot several landings and each one was smooth and right on target. As we returned to the flight line an officer from the maintenance sub-depot approached us with a broken L casting, the part to which the wheel is attached.

The top half of the casting was corroded, indicating it had been cracked previously. Seeing the faulty part, the colonel turned to me, shook my hand and said, "Tomorrow I will return your salute as a fellow officer." The next day my mother proudly pinned on my wings.

I'd flown twenty-two missions with those Second Louie bars. After covering them with the white tape I climbed into the plane and took my place in the cockpit.

Williamson and I went through the routine check, questioning the crew about the condition of their guns, supply of ammunition, and individual equipment. The engines were started.

When we were taxiing for takeoff, I heard someone calling on the intercom.

"Right waist to pilot. Over."

"Go ahead."

"My harness is too tight and won't fasten. Over."

Dick in the cockpit of his B-17

"Check the radio room. Should be another one there."

"Roger."

I was concerned about the new right waist gunner. I had not seen him until this morning and couldn't remember his name. A harness was a crucial part of every crew member's flight uniform and was usually fastened over our heavy flight jackets before boarding the airplane. The chest pack, which held the parachute, was too bulky to wear in flight; in an emergency it would be fastened on the harness at the last minute.

"Pilot to ball turret. Help the right waist into his harness. Report back. Over."

"Roger."

A few minutes later Reiss reported that the new waist gunner had found a harness and it was in place. We had not had occasion to abandon our plane, nor did we plan to do so, but we were always prepared.

Taxiing out to the rough metal runway, we were the next to last plane in our squadron to take off. After the plane left the ground, we banked in a shallow climbing turn and rendezvoused into formation. Tail-end Charlie was slightly behind and below. There were only a few clouds as we turned north and headed for the Adriatic. The throbbing of the four engines became our pulse and heartbeat.

Once over the water the gunners test-fired their guns. Their skill and accuracy were our main protection from enemy fighters. Periodically Williamson and I checked the oil pressure and engine temperatures and synchronized all four engines. As we reached 8,000 feet, I instructed the crew to put on their oxygen masks.

We continued to climb and leveled off at 21,500 feet. It was about 20 degrees below zero at this altitude and we were thankful for our sheepskin lined jackets and pants.

Waist Gunner Cecil Sullivant

I always had butterflies before a mission, but after we were in the air, flying the plane required intense concentration and I didn't have time to be scared. As the attack on Udine was to be made from the north, we were to fly into southern Austria before beginning the bomb run. After making a long sweeping turn south, I adjusted our heading to reach the IP (Initial Point). When we were about 30 minutes from the target the top turret reported a group of planes in the distance. Could they be our "little friends," arriving to give support?

As the planes flew closer, Spoon in the top turret called, "Bandits approaching at six o'clock high." The planes we were to bomb at Udine were in the air, not on the ground!

"Tail gunner to pilot. Eight FW 190's at six o'clock level. Over."

Immediately there was a sharp burst under the left wing as eight silver Focke-Wulfs came streaking by in pairs from port side and behind the clock. The FWs were firing rockets at a range our .50 caliber guns couldn't match. When their shells hit our plane, they exploded into thousands of fragments, almost like flak. Each second of time had a rocket shell in it.

"Pilot to crew. Let's knock those Jerries out of the sky before they get us. Over."

As the fighters passed again at a high rate of closure, the guns of our crew went into action. The pungent smell of burnt powder filled our cockpit and the ship shuddered to the recoil of waist, nose, and ball-turret guns. Orange flashes followed the enemy projectiles as they twisted and hurtled down toward the group below us. I saw pieces fly off the wing of one of the fighters before they passed from view.

Curry cried out, "Got one of them fighters."

Just as I was silently congratulating Curry, he yelled over the intercom, "Jeez, Number 10 has had it!"

Tail-end Charlie had fallen out of formation. The B-17 was a mass of flames.

"See any chutes?"

"1, ... 2, ... 3, ... 4... 5.

The plane behind us plunged madly downward, spiraling and smoking in its death struggle.

It took a lot of guts for a fighter pilot to enter a bomber formation with its concentrated fire power. Consequently, a squadron of fighters often attacked the most vulnerable planes, those at the tail-end of the combat box, often referred to as the coffin corner.

With tail-end Charlie gone, we were the trailing ship in the last element — seven enemy fighters against one Flying Fortress. There was no time to be scared; I had to give all my attention to keep the ship level and pray that our gunners would get those bandits before they got us. Maintaining formation was crucial. We could not dodge nor change position. We were a clay duck on the wrong end of an aerial shooting gallery. Curry reported through the intercom that the fighters were returning, flying above and behind us, to the right, just far enough out so our guns couldn't reach them.

Like wolves attacking a wounded deer the FWs swooped down on us. Suddenly a ball of fire shot through the air, landing on our left wing just between the two engines. Our ship began to vibrate and quiver.

Reiss, in the ball turret, saw a great gaping hole in the wing with gasoline spewing out. He climbed out of the turret, yelling to the waist gunners, "We're goners. The plane is about to explode!"

Cletus Reiss in the Ball Turret

Marion shouted, "Let's get the hell out of here."

Smoke was penetrating the cockpit as I desperately tried to feather the engine, but the motor failed to cooperate. The propeller spun out of control, causing the left wing to drop. I kicked hard on the right rudder and set the trim tabs as far to the right as possible in a frenzied last effort to level out our damaged ship.

"Pilot to crew. Prepare to bail out."

"Tail gunner to pilot. Here they come again!"

The gunners opened fire and one of the attacking FWs spiraled down, leaving its smoke path behind.

The Focke-Wulf's rockets pierced our right wing and exploded. A piece shrapnel cut my right arm. The ship still held to the right, and the fire began to spread over both wings as smoke and fire came from the instrument panel, shorting out the controls. We were gradually losing altitude and had to leave the formation. In time, the fire would reach the tanks. Then it would be all over for us. To steady the plane, I put it on automatic pilot and called on the intercom,

'Pilot to crew. Bail out! Bail out!"

Hearing the command, Marion tore through the narrow waist of the plane, accidentally knocking down both Brown and Sully as they were fastening their chest packs. Marion had mentally prepared himself on previous missions; if the occasion for bailing out presented itself he would jump immediately.

7

After opening the door, he discovered he had neglected to put on his chest pack. Hurrying back to retrieve it, he tore past the men again. Still, Marion was the first crew member to leave the plane.

Reiss was the second man to jump out of the waist escape hatch. Brown and Sullivant quickly followed as Spoon dropped through the bomb bay. Tail gunner Curry found the tail hatch jammed, so he crawled up to the waist. It was deserted. He found the waist hatch open and jumped. In the meantime, the engineer, bombardier, navigator, and copilot had jumped from ether the nose hatch or bomb bay.

By now the ship was vibrating excessively from the runaway engine and the left wing dropped dangerously and sharply as the fire began consuming the entire plane. I was concerned about Reiss. Had he heard my command to bail out? I had called on the intercom several times but now with the fire all communication was lost.

Seeing no one in the fore part of the ship, I stepped down to the catwalk by the bomb bay and said good-bye to our faithful #472, thankful she had given everyone time to leave. In my flight training I had practiced flying formation and bombing, but we did not practice bailing out of an aircraft at nineteen thousand feet. The first time had to be the right one. I looked at my watch. The time was 1005. I closed my eyes and tumbled forward.

After abandoning the plane, I counted to ten, then reached with my right hand to pull the rip cord. It wasn't there! Panic stricken, I reached on my left side. Saying a prayer, I found it and pulled the cord. In my haste I had snapped my parachute on upside down. As my chute opened, I looked back and saw our plane twisting down in a sickening spiral, consumed by a fountain of fire.

With the parachute open, my fall was broken. My first sensation was a feeling of relief. Surprisingly, I was not conscious of falling, but rather was surrounded with a sense of peace. I felt as though I was suspended in the air and time had stopped. Any dreams of escape were shattered when I saw one of the FW 190s circling around me. The pilot waved and turned his plane so I was behind his tail. The air stream from his propeller hit my parachute and swung me back and forth. At first, I thought he planned to shoot me, but realized he was radioing my position to the Germans on the ground, so they could capture me.[2]

---

[2] The pilot may also have been documenting his kill with gun-cameras, and a little "sport." By doing this, the pilot stays behind the bomber formation. Or, he may have been out of fuel and was making a pass on his way home.

I looked down. It was a clear day. I could see the blue Adriatic and, near the water, a city surrounded by rugged mountains. Drawing closer I noticed German jeeps driving back and forth on the road below. They were already looking for our crew.

Suddenly the ground started coming up fast and there was a mountain lake to skirt. Landing in the frigid water with heavy sheepskin-lined clothing would put a quick end to all my problems. Pulling the strings of the parachute to avoid landing there, I fell on the rocky shore and blacked out. When I opened my eyes, I looked up into the faces of five or six people who had gathered around me. The men carried guns and one of them questioned me, "Deutsch?"

I was confused. I mumbled something in English. The men helped me out of my parachute and handed it to one of the women. As I stood up, I discovered I had banged up my right knee. It was painful, but I could walk.

One of the men motioned to me to follow him. We walked a short distance and entered a small cabin where I was taken to an elderly man who could speak broken English. For years the old fellow had worked in the coal mines of Pennsylvania and made enough money to return to his native country where he was living out his last years. He asked me questions.

"Is Coolidge still President?"

"Did the Yanks win the World Series?"

He was curious about the United States, visiting with me until he was confident that I was one of the Allies and not a German spy. Before long a man with a red star sewn on his cap appeared. I was greatly relieved, for we had been told in our briefings that we should look for the Partisans who could be identified by a red star. I was now in the hands of Tito's underground.

The man who was to be my guide was thickset and stalwart, with typical Slavic features. He wore a beard but appeared to be fairly young, no more than 30. Taking out the cloth map from my escape kit, I tried to find out where I was. The guide pointed to an area northwest of Fiume.

I figured the city I had seen from the air before landing was Fiume, a town well controlled by the Germans. It was Lady Luck who had brought me to this mountainous area where I should be safe for a time. Knowing about the war department regulation that prevented evadees from carrying a gun, I gave my 45 to the Partisan guide. He motioned for me to follow him. The trail was rocky and rough, and I limped along nursing my sore knee. We walked until almost dusk.

The trail led to Sarconi, a small village where we stopped to rest. Entering a small house, I was elated to find another American airman. Since I didn't recognize him, I assumed he was a member of another crew. As we visited, I discovered he was Bob Brown, the new waist gunner who had been assigned to Churchill's position.

"Weren't you the guy whose harness didn't fit?" I asked.

"Yes sir," said Brown. "Lucky for me Sully found one that would fasten over these heavy pants."

"Been in Italy long?"

"No, sir. We flew into the base only four days ago. Didn't suppose I'd use my parachute on my first mission."

"Sorry we couldn't accommodate you with a successful mission," I said, "but you'll have to admit we've given you a bit of excitement. You new fellows were assigned to us so we could teach you the ropes of flying in combat. We forgot to tell you, Brown, that the ropes could be attached to a parachute!"

I was responsible for the men in my plane, and it was gratifying to find the first member of my crew. Brown and I were taken to another small cabin where several men wore bill caps, each with a red star. Going outside to use the facilities I saw two men coming toward the house. One was in U.S. uniform; the man following him carried a gun and was pulling a wagon with large wooden wheels. Inside was an airman. Could these men be more of our crew?

As the first fellow came closer, he yelled out, "Hey, that you Munsen?" Reiss, my ball turret gunner, greeted me with a broad grin. Slapping me on the back he said, "And this was supposed to be a milk run?" Turning around we saw the Yugoslav pulling the wagon towards the door of the cabin. He lifted his patient and placed him carefully on the floor inside. It was then I realized the airman was Thomas Howard, the bombardier who had joined our crew that morning. We had met only a few hours ago during briefing. "I must have broken my goddamn ankle when I landed," Howard said. "You fellows have any pain killer? This ankle hurts like hell. I've used my morphine."

Our survival kits contained some sulfa powder, morphine, a chocolate bar, compass, cigarettes, $50 in script, and cloth maps with which to identify our location. Brown and I gave Howard both the morphine and sulfa powder from our kits. Reiss was repeating his story about meeting him.

"After landing in the mountains, I was trying to reach an old dirt road below and heard someone cry out, 'Over here — over here! I need help!' "

10

"Investigating I found this fellow crawling and dragging his leg, writhing in pain. His ankle appeared to be broken. I discovered he was one of our men — our new navigator, in fact, so I picked him up and carried him a quarter mile or so. By then I was damn near exhausted, so I put him down to rest."

"While we were sitting on this hill, I'm wondering what I'm going to do with this guy with a bad ankle. And then we see this man coming toward us with a rifle. Howard gives me his 45 and I put it under my flight jacket. If this guy proved to be unfriendly, he would soon have a great big hole in his gut."

"As I'm sitting with the gun under my coat — pointed right at him, he takes off his hat and shows us the red star. When I pulled my hand out and the guy realized he'd been under the gun all that time, his eyes got big as saucers. Good thing he showed his red star when he did. He's the guy that got the 45."

Our visiting was interrupted as one of the Partisans brought over a bottle of wine and an egg in the shell for each of us. First to break his egg, Brown discovered to everyone's amazement that it was raw. We were puzzled by our hosts' idea of a culinary treat.

"Ever eat a raw egg?" asked Brown.

Reiss was holding his nose. "Not on your life."

Gulping down the raw egg with the wine I said, "But we can't offend our hosts." Reiss claimed the wine was laced with kerosene and made him sicker than a poisoned pup. The combination of the wine and raw egg spoiled our appetites for the good meal offered later.

After dark, two other Partisans arrived and motioned to us to go outside. A cold, icy wind was blowing from the north, and we were thankful for our sheepskin-lined pants and jackets. Trudging single file up the mountain path, we wondered why we couldn't have stayed in the warmth of the cabin below. Exhausted after three or four hours of walking, we welcomed the little mountain hut that was our destination.

There were three of us: Reiss, Brown, and me. Howard, not able to walk, remained behind in the cabin where we had spent the afternoon.

I wondered what Brown and Howard were thinking. What a way to indoctrinate them into the air war over Europe — being hit by a German Jerry on their first mission. But their anxiety could have been no greater than those of us with more experience. First or 23rd mission, none of us were prepared for this. Landing in German occupied territory we were all fugitives, forced to fight for survival. I was concerned about Howard. I wondered if we'd ever see him again.

We stumbled into the small hut, thankful for the protection it provided from the cruel wind. The guides built a fire in the middle of the room on the dirty floor. They stretched out and immediately fell asleep while we tried to find a comfortable position on the narrow benches built around the walls of the room.

The wind blew through the cracks. With no chimney flue the fire gave off more smoke than heat. I started coughing and my eyes were watering. I longed to be safe in our little tent on the base back in Amendola — the one I had cursed so often.

Our base had been in operation only five days when we landed there in late January. The first two nights my men had no cots and slept on the ground. For warmth we improvised stoves from used oil drums — risky devices that exploded on occasion, once burning my hand. During storms we got up at night, put on coats and in the freezing wind and rain struggled to hold down the tent. Facilities were primitive at Amendola, but at least we were safe from capture by the Germans.

In this country, not so. Today we had escaped the enemy, but those fighter pilots had radioed our position and they'd be looking for us tomorrow. Could these impoverished Partisans really help us?

Events of the day tumbled through my head — the formation of fighters descending on us, the ball of fire that hit our plane, the parachute jump and then not being able to find my rip cord. I was scared to death when the fire in the plane shorted out the electrical and control systems, and in my hurry, I evidently snapped the chest pack on upside down. That's what made it open with my left hand. If the chute hadn't opened it would have been curtains for me. I was lucky to be alive.

I turned over to warm my hind end and noticed that the new waist gunner was also restless. The haze and smoke bothered him, too, and he seemed eager to talk. I asked him about his parachute drop. "One of those Focke-Wulf pilots followed me down," recalled Brown. "The force from his propeller swung me and scared the hell out of me. He was so close I could see him wave at me! In seconds he was gone, and it was all very quiet, peacefully quiet after the deafening roar of our plane's engines and the gunfire."

"When did you find out your harness wouldn't fasten?"

"Not until after we were rendezvousing. My harness had been fit for an electric flying suit. With no electric suits in the supply room, I had to put my harness over this bulky flight suit and it wouldn't fasten. It was Sully who told me I'd better find one that fit. The one I found in the radio room was tight, too, so tight it almost cut off my circulation. But I was damn lucky to have it on!"

"When I jumped, I knew I had to count to ten, to be free of the plane before opening the chute. After my chute opened, I thought I'd died and gone to heaven or something. The damn harness straps were so tight when I pulled them, I didn't think I had any legs. I couldn't figure out what was going on."

"First was the deafening noise of the engines and the guns — and then suddenly bailing out into complete silence. I thought I was dead. I actually heard celestial sounds, like angels singing. It seemed like a dream — and I couldn't believe it was really me. Until I hit a tree, I don't think it ever did dawn on me what was happening."

"You landed in a tree?"

"I was lucky. A tree broke my fall. In that forest I chose a tall evergreen, landing high up in the tree, about 12 to 15 feet above the ground. My chute was tangled in the branches and I spent quite a little time figuring out how in the hell I was going to get out of there. It was when I was in the tree I saw this guy walking up, and then I got out of that chute in a hurry. I finally worked myself loose, got the chute out of the tree and buried it under the snow."

Brown continued, "Oh God, I was scared after landing. This guy walked toward me. From his uniform I was sure he was a Jerry. I stopped and picked up a rock. When I got up to him, he showed me the red star. Then I knew I was with the Partisans. Since I couldn't understand a word, he was saying I took out my map. He pointed to the place we were and motioned for me to follow him."

I stood up to warm myself by the fire. "The Focke-Wulf pilot who waved at you was radioing our position to German intelligence. We may be safe here in the mountains tonight, but when daylight comes the Germans will be hot on our trail."

I wondered how the Partisans and others could sleep. The smoke was almost choking me. But more important I wondered where the other members of the crew might be. Had they been picked up by the Partisans — or captured by the Germans?

We thanked God we had landed safely. The days ahead would demand the ultimate from our strength and stamina. The mountains would be both our taskmaster and our salvation.

DAY TWO • SUNDAY • MARCH 19

I must have dozed, for one of the Partisans shook me and indicated it was time to get up. The fire was out and the air had cleared, but my hands and feet were numb and my knee was stiff. Reiss and Brown were jumping up and down trying to keep warm while I moved my arms in a frenzied kind of way to get my circulation going. It was five o'clock and still dark.

We followed our guides on a rough path, bordered by tall, ghost-like trees. The wind had died down and walking was easier; the tautness in my thighs told me that we were going downhill.

Each of us was deep in his own thoughts. Were the Partisans trustworthy? Could these fellows get us past the German patrols? If only one of us could understand their language. We knew this was Sunday, March 19. We knew the time of day by looking at a watch, but no one knew where we were or where we were going. We found ourselves asking questions none of us could answer.

"Where in the hell are we?"

"Someone talked about Kastav. Where on God's earth is that?" "I heard them say Fiume. Must be near the Adriatic."

Always questions, but no answers. Our instructions during briefing were to follow the Partisans implicitly. So, we trudged on, placing one foot in front of the other, following the fellow ahead, hoping we would soon be returned to our base. We had no other choice. Brown turned around and asked, "Don't these fellows ever eat?"

We were all ravenous, but we hoped there'd be no more raw eggs with wine. In the dim light of dawn, I noticed the trees were thinning out and we were approaching a village. The guides knocked on the door of one of the houses and hustled us into a small room, barely large enough for the six of us.

Our Yugoslav hosts passed a bottle of rakija, a plum brandy which seemed to be a common beverage in this country. They toasted one another by crying, "Zdravo!" which we soon learned meant "Health to you!" The woman of the house brought in something resembling bread. We picked it up hungrily. As we ate, bits of straw got stuck in our teeth. It didn't satisfy our appetite and before long we were ravenously hungry again. But talk was cheap, and we were anxious to share experiences. Reiss's voice came through loud and clear.

"I jumped out the hatch right after Marion. I didn't free-fall. I pulled that rip cord about two seconds after I jumped. If that chute wasn't going to open, I

15

wanted to know it, for I intended to claw that sucker open. The slip stream opened the chute."

"I've always had to take the padding off the back of my harness because I couldn't get into the turret without that extra inch of room. I'll tell you, when that chute opened, I knew why that harness was padded. Those straps dug into my armpits like knives, and I must have passed out for awhile. Bailing out at 19,000 feet, I may have had some oxygen problems, too."

"It was bitter cold, and I'm wondering: Why am I holding onto the rip cord? It evidently gave me a sense of security to hold on to that damn thing, and I literally had to force myself to drop the cord. When I dropped it out halfway down, I felt I was doing something real wrong. At the same time a German fighter pilot turned his plane so the prop wash would hit me and cause me to swing. I was sure he was going to shoot me. Oh, God, was I scared!

"While I was floating down, I knew I'd land in enemy-occupied territory. I knew there'd be no post offices, telephones, or anything like that. I couldn't say to my mother, 'Hey, I'm OK.' I knew it would probably be weeks before she'd know if I'm OK or not, so I just said the most fervent prayer I've ever said in my life: 'Oh, God, let my mother know that I'm all right.'"[3]

"Suddenly the ground started to come up real fast and I hit the side of a cliff. I kept kicking myself away, but like a pendulum I came right back again. I must have torn the hell out of my kidneys for I've had to take a leak every ten minutes since I landed."

Voices became dim and I wasn't hearing what Reiss said. The tension of combat, the encounter with the Partisans, the climb to the mountain hut, the fear of capture by the Germans had all taken their toll. I stretched out on one of the benches.

I awakened to the sounds of laughter and excited jabbering. It was late afternoon. A few more people had entered the small room and a familiar voice carried above the others.

"Reiss, I thought you were still in that damn ball turret!"

"Spoon, how the devil did you get here?"

"Just like you — these guys with the red stars saved my ass. Who's that in the corner? Old son-of-a-gun Munsen. Hey, how about passing the schnapps."

---

[3]Later Cletus heard that his mother awoke the night of March 18 and called out, "Buddy is calling me." Turning to her husband she said, "Something has happened to Buddy, but he's all right."

I got up and greeted my faithful engineer, thankful to see another one of my crew safe. Everyone was talking at once. Spoon was wearing an odd-looking coonskin cap and I wondered why and where he found such bizarre headgear.

"How'd you come by that Daniel Boone cap? Carry it down with you from the plane?"

"Hell, no. It's covering up my brains."

Spoon took off his cap and we saw a rag covered with blood. There was a large gash in his skull.

I was shocked. "We've got to make these people understand you need to see a doctor."

"Not on your life. I'm not taking any goddamn chances of being left behind. I'll get along. I've poured on that sulfa powder, and I'll find some more. This damn wood alcohol, or whatever it is, will keep me going 'til they get us out of here."

"How'd you get hurt?"

"When smoke started pouring out of the engine, I knew the doggone plane would blow up any time. When you ordered us to bail out, I grabbed my chute pack, fastened it and headed for the closest exit — the bomb bay. Soon as I jumped, I felt a terrible blow on my head. About knocked me out. Guess I hit the corner of the bomb bay."

"That was a hell of a ride hanging from a parachute. My head was pounding all the way down. When I landed, blood was oozing down my face."

"A couple of them guys with red stars on their caps came by, rolled up my parachute, and took me to a small cabin. My head was pounding, but I was going to damn well find out where I was and get the hell out of there. The two men were babbling and pointing to my head. As I got out my map to find out where I was, a woman brought a piece of cloth and laid it on my head. She'd found this crazy Daniel Boone cap and put it on top to keep the rag in place. The men gave me something to drink. I don't know what kind of booze they have over here but it's powerful. After a couple of drinks, I guess the natives decided I was ready to travel!"

"We were in the mountains, snow on the ground and it was hellish cold. I dragged behind those guys, following in their footsteps for hours. By evening we reached a village, and it was there they took me to the house where I slept. I still don't know where the hell I've been, or where this godforsaken place is!"

17

Spoon was interrupted by a knock at the door. With loud cheers we greeted two more of our group. One of the fellows was Bill Seward, our navigator whom I had met for the first time yesterday morning. Less than 30 hours after bailing out, I could account for six of the ten in my crew.

Seward introduced us to Gordon. By now the room was crowded and everyone was talking at once. In conversation with Gordon I discovered he was a copilot in our squadron. Trained as a P-38 fighter pilot, he had requested a transfer to a four-engine plane when he was sent to Italy. After ten hours of training in a B-17 he started flying missions and flew with anyone who needed a copilot.

Sitting down next to Spoon, Gordon recalled, "I was flying with Adams on the Udine mission."

"So, you were tail-end Charlie," interrupted Brown.

Reiss chimed in, "I saw those Jerries rip you apart."

"Our ship was attacked by eight FW 190s," explained Gordon. "I heard an explosion. Fragments from the exploding rocket hit the windshield and the flying glass cut my face. When Adams saw the fire on our left wing near the inboard engine, he gave the order to bail out."

Gordon knew he had our full attention, so he leaned back and told about his experiences.

"While I reached under the seat for my chest pack, one of the crew called through the intercom that the escape hatch wouldn't open. Adams reached under his seat for his parachute, couldn't find it, and jumped down to the catwalk to retrieve it. He joined the engineer and Doran, our navigator, and the three managed to force the door open. During the commotion the plane was rapidly losing altitude. I leveled off, re-trimmed the aircraft, turned off the master switches and climbed down to follow them. Pulling off my oxygen mask, I pushed the door open against the strong wind and jumped."

"I didn't count to ten but pulled the rip cord immediately. As I floated down my harness kept sliding up, binding me under my armpits. Woozy with pain I had no sensation of time. Suddenly the ground came up fast and I landed on my back, hitting some rough rocks."

"After pulling in my chute, I unhooked the harness shoulder strap, relieved to get rid of the pressure under my arms. I carefully folded my chute and hid it under a rock. Reaching down to disconnect the leg straps of the harness, I discovered they were hanging loose. They had never been fastened!

The only reason I hadn't fallen out of the parachute harness was because in my hurry I had put my Mae West over the chute. The crotch strap from the Mae West had saved my life! I took a deep breath and said a prayer. The good Lord was looking after me."

"Digging into my pockets for material that shouldn't fall into enemy hands, I found my note book with flight information and tore it up. I took my compass out of the escape kit, hoping it would be of some help in the mountains."

Mae West was slang for Life Preserver

"Starting to climb down to lower ground, I kept from falling by holding onto branches of young trees. The incline was too steep, so I climbed back up to try a different route. From the top I had a good view of the area and spotted a German airdrome. The hangers looked as if they were built into the side of a mountain. I knew I was near an area heavily controlled by the Germans, so I had to keep moving."

"Climbing down the opposite side I did a double take when seven heads appeared above me. As the men became visible, I could see rifles slung over their uniforms. Finding a crevice between two rocks I hid, hoping my khaki colored flying suit would blend into the rocks. The soldiers were headed in my direction. I held my breath as they walked on down the mountain and passed only a few feet from me."

"I waited a few minutes. With an airdrome nearby, I couldn't take chances. As I worked my way down the hill, I heard footsteps behind me. Time and again I would hide, look, and listen... Everything was quiet. It was just my imagination."

"After reaching a gully I climbed another hill. Halfway up I saw a fellow wearing a leather jacket over his powder blue flight suit. When I caught up with him, I found out he was Sgt. Kuch, tail gunner on Adams' plane. Since this was my first mission with Adams, I hadn't recognized the sergeant, but I could see he was bleeding and in trouble. Kuch's injuries were severe. He was hit by rocket fire from the Focke-Wulf fighters who attacked us; a piece of shrapnel had penetrated his right heel and elbow. His right arm was bleeding profusely, and his heel was so badly shattered he limped with pain. To stem the flow of blood, I applied a tourniquet above the elbow and gave him the morphine in my escape kit."

19

"Kuch told me that he had also seen soldiers. He was relieved when he saw red stars on their caps and realized they were Partisans. They helped him at first, but because of his injuries he could scarcely walk. The leader was in a hurry and they left him in the mountains."

"Knowing we were close to the Adriatic I was leery about encountering Germans, so we waited, hoping the Partisans would return to give us assistance in the downhill climb. Kuch explained he had talked with the soldiers in German, a language he had known from his youth. If the soldiers were Partisans, I wondered why they hadn't returned. Had they suspected Kuch was a German?"

"Kuch was in danger of freezing to death so we started to follow the tracks in the snow left by the soldiers. With support he was able to limp along, dragging his right leg. The pain was intense, and he was forced to stop often. Weak from the loss of blood, Kuch said repeatedly, 'Lieutenant, I can't go on any further. This is about it.' I washed his face with snow and cold seemed to revive him. Somehow I was able to drag and pull Kuch until we reached the valley."

"It was growing dark. We were desperate to find shelter. In the dim light I thought I saw a house in the distance. Leaving Kuch by the trail I took off to investigate. Coming nearer I realized what had appeared to be a house was only a large boulder. My mind was playing tricks on me again. Exhausted, I walked back to Kuch. While waiting he had noticed a wisp of smoke rising above the trees farther down the valley."

"I half carried, half dragged Kuch down the trail. Seeing a glimmer of light, we headed toward it. There was a house, and outside was a woman doing chores. When she saw us, she covered her mouth with her hand, muffling a cry. We pointed to the house and she led us to the door. Though he knew German, Kuch was afraid to speak the language for fear she would think we were Germans. Entering the home, we saw a man with dark hair and stocky frame. He looked at us with piercing, questioning eyes."

"Noticing Kuch's injuries, the woman found a place for him to lie down and tried to make him comfortable. Wanting to thank her, Kuch finally spoke to her in German. The lady smiled and he explained we were American airmen looking for the Partisans. Her husband frowned and obviously was not happy to have us in his home. There was much talking, and he finally left the house."

"The woman soaked Kuch's arm in warm water until she could remove his blood-soaked jacket. After wrapping his wounds in clean cloths, she offered us both warm milk, the first either of us had since we left the States. To show our appreciation we shared the chocolate in our escape kits with the four little children. They were delighted. One of the little boys climbed up on my lap and looked in my pockets, searching for more."

"While playing with the children, we heard the tramping of heavy boots outside the house. The man had returned with several men. To our great relief they wore red stars on their caps. Again, we were quizzed, Kuch answering them in German. After lots of talking, two men took a blanket, pulled it taut and nailed it onto two logs. Kuch winced with pain as they lifted him on this homemade stretcher. But realizing he wouldn't have to walk was a great relief to him. From the conversation Kuch gathered that German scouts were only a mile away. It was more luck than sense that we had walked in on a family sympathetic to our cause."

"With the Partisans carrying Kuch, we walked to the other side of the village. There we met Seward who had been hiding with another family. The network of communication among these Partisans was awesome, but most amazing was how they knew every move the Germans made and were able to evade them. Leaving the village, we headed for the mountains. The Partisans took turns carrying Kuch on the homemade stretcher. I found out that Seward, here, was a navigator on Munsen's plane and the same Focke-Wulfs that shot us down also got their plane."

"Arriving in another village we stopped at a cottage where one of the natives spoke English. He gave us some schnapps that must have been homemade, for it burned all the way down. We soon learned why the Partisans had stopped for a breather. They knew we had a two-hour trek ahead of us. Since the schnapps had not eased Kuch's pain, Seward gave him the morphine from his kit to make him more comfortable.

"When we left the warmth and protection of the cottage it was almost midnight, fourteen hours since I had bailed out. Exhausted from the day's events, I blindly followed the guides. The night was dark, with no moon. A raw wind whipped through our clothing. I don't know which was worse — the cold, the fatigue, my aching back or the hunger."

"Our guides were quiet as they entered the next village. Once again, we found refuge in a small house. Lying down on a bench along one wall I fell asleep immediately. In a short time, we were awakened and told we would start walking again. When we left the house, it was still dark; looking at my watch I saw it was three in the morning."

Apparently, these Partisans can go days with little food or rest. Their stamina and the sacrifices they made for us were incredible. It was all I could do to walk, and these guys were taking turns carrying Kuch on the stretcher.

"We were in the mountains and had rough trails to climb. Seward and I followed the fellows carrying the stretcher. At times it required extra hands to manipulate the turns. Fortunately, Kuch was no longer complaining of pain, so the morphine was doing its job. Impossible to see the path ahead in the dark, I stumbled over rocks and fell down time after time. The going got rougher and I was panting to keep up with the guides. Finally, I put my arms around two of the Partisans, and with their support managed to continue."

"Climbing higher and higher, Seward and I felt we couldn't continue the pace. Leaving the group for a few minutes, two of the Partisans returned with a flat-topped wagon they had found beside an old hut. Seward and I crawled into the wagon and rode down the mountain trails, guided by the Partisans. I marveled how they managed to brake that wagon repeatedly, with us as cargo."

"Our guides must have felt we were out of danger because they started singing as we followed the winding trail down the mountain. Their jolly spirit helped to raise our morale. Reaching a small village before daylight, we noticed that several of the houses had been burned. After finding one that was intact, the Partisans took us inside, built a fire and moved Kuch carefully onto a large bed. Seward and I squeezed in beside him. Before going to sleep I heard voices in the next room and could see the people pointing at us. American airmen were evidently a novelty."

"We slept almost all day. When we woke, we showed the Partisans our escape maps and they pointed to a place a little northeast of Fiume not far from the Adriatic. When they told Kuch there were other Americans nearby, we asked to see them. Kuch would have liked to shoot the breeze with all of you."

When Gordon had finished his account, I looked around at my crew — Brown, Reiss, Spoon and Seward — thankful for the five of us who had survived and hopefully could follow whatever route the Partisans would take. I wondered about the injured — Kuch and my bombardier, Howard. Would they get out of Yugoslavia alive? And where were my other men? What accidents or injury may have befallen them? As darkness set in, Gordon and Seward's guide motioned it was time to go. Our guides, too, were preparing to take us to another house for the night. Apparently, it was safer to move under the cover of darkness.

DAY THREE • MONDAY • MARCH 20

Today was Monday. Four of us had spent the night sleeping on wooden benches in a cellar. We were surrounded by the family's most precious possessions — food, mainly carrots and potatoes — and wine.

We had entered the room in the black of night through a crawl space below ground level. The same opening was used by the man who brought us water and polenta, or cornmeal mush, for breakfast. From his conversation we gathered we were in the town of Kosi. He asked for our names and serial numbers for use as passports. I wrote down the information for our group which included Reiss, Brown, Spoon and me. Howard, in need of medical attention, had stayed at the farmhouse we visited the first afternoon. We hoped the Partisan doctors could care for him.

Evading capture meant moving frequently and we were grateful the Partisans were able to find people willing to help us. During a period of less than 48 hours, I had been in five homes or huts, proof the Germans were scouring the countryside looking for us. Those who offered us shelter were exposing themselves and their families to the danger of reprisals — even death — at the hands of their captors. I wondered if families in my home town in Iowa would risk their lives by hiding Yugoslavs if their lives were endangered.

Time passed slowly. Our inability to communicate left us frustrated and completely isolated. Even if we had known their language, the Partisans would probably not have revealed their plans to us. Worried about our plight, we could do nothing but wait for their next move.

While shooting the breeze we took turns visiting the outdoor facilities; the straw bread was good for something. Waiting for Brown to return we heard someone calling, "Nirnski!, Nitnski!," As Brown crawled through the narrow opening he whispered, "It's the Germans!"

"Did they see you?"

"I don't know, but they're coming."

Spoon couldn't miss a good pun. "Brown, you almost got caught with your pants down!"

Our attention was drawn to loud voices in the room above us. We could hear feet stomping and boots clicking — proof the Germans were there. In this little house there were few places to hide. Each of us harbored our own fears.

23

If the Germans found us, we knew our future. We would be taken prisoners and sit out the remainder of the war in a POW camp. I was more concerned about the family giving us shelter. They could be shot and other families in the village killed as well. With great relief we heard the tramping diminish and the door close.

This was only a hint of what was to come. We were to discover we would always have the Germans on our heels. They had an uncanny sixth sense about the Partisans' activities. Likewise, the Partisans, with their scouts and cunning, were well aware of the enemy's movements. When the guide entered our hiding place, his motions told us we would have to leave. We could not endanger the family any longer. Outside the wind was harsh and cold; we knew there would be another long walk ahead of us.

As we were leaving, the woman of the house gave us coarse bread and cheese to put into our pockets. We smiled and nodded, trying to convey our gratitude to these courageous people who had protected us from the Germans and shared some of their precious food. We followed our Partisan guide silently through the village. Because it was still daylight any movement was visible to villagers and German scouts alike.

Approaching the tree covered hills we met Gordon and Seward, who were also forced to leave their hiding place. Spoon described our recent scare with the Germans. Gordon said Kuch heard the Partisans had killed two German soldiers. The villagers feared reprisals and expected each house would be searched. We hoped the Germans wouldn't find Kuch who had to stay behind because of his injuries. The Partisans would take him, when it was safe, to a Partisan hospital. Tito's underground was more organized and far-reaching than we had been led to believe from our indoctrination lectures.

In case we had to bail out, Major Benjamin had given us instructions for contacting the underground. Yugoslavia, he said, had two organized resistance units that provided escape routes for downed Allied airmen, the Partisans and Chetniks. The major explained how they could be identified, but we knew nothing about the civil war going on between the two groups.

Walking single file behind our guide, we noticed dark clouds to the north. Terrified from the brief encounter with the Germans, we walked silently through the pine trees. Soon the trail went downhill. Stumbling along the steep incline, we were hoping the rain would hold off until we reached our destination.

Although darkness afforded protection we were left with a feeling of hopelessness and despair as we blindly followed the fellow in front of us. I wondered when my folks would receive the message about my missing-in-action status. I knew Mother would interpret the term, "missing in action," as "killed in action." If there were only some way a message could be sent to tell her I was all right.

I recalled Mother and the tears she shed that day in Kearney, Nebraska, when we said our good-byes. My crew and I had been sent to Kearney to pick up our plane and Dad and Mother had driven from Iowa to meet me there. I couldn't reveal my orders, but each of us knew I would soon be going overseas. We had walked out to the field where the new B-17s were parked, waiting for their crews. Dad was impressed with the size of the four-engine bombers and proud that his son would be in command of one of these prestigious Flying Fortresses.

We had celebrated my 22nd birthday in the motel where the folks were staying. Mother surprised me by bringing one of her prize-winning angel food cakes, frosted with a thin layer of icing. She placed candles on top, lit them and she and Dad sang "Happy Birthday." I knew what Mother and Dad were thinking — that this could be our last time together. I was confident, however, that the overseas trip was just another hurdle to cross. But the hurdle was a bit more than I had anticipated. Everything had happened so fast after the Focke-Wulfs hit us that we were still in a bit of shock.

The walking had become easier as we reached a valley and followed the path alongside a river. Starved for food, Reiss, Brown, Spoon and I dug into our pockets and pulled out some of the bread and cheese given us earlier. Gordon and Seward had also received food, but they had real meat! When they shared it with us we realized it tasted just like chicken. A pet rabbit, they said — succulent, tender and delicious. We were overtaken with gratitude for the sacrifices these poor families had made for us.

Approaching a village our guide rapped on the door of one of the houses and was permitted to enter. Expecting this to be our destination we were disappointed to see our guide return with more Partisans. So, our trip for the night was not over. Our disappointment, however, quickly turned to cheers as the door of the house opened again and we saw five men dressed in U.S. Air Force flight suits. Three were from my crew: Vern Curry, Irv Williamson and Cecil Sullivant.

Williamson, my copilot, grabbed my arm and exclaimed, "Some milk run, Munsen!" Curry wore a broad grin and Sully joined in the joyful pandemonium. In just two and a half days all my crew was accounted for except the radio operator, Marion, who was the first to bail out of the ship. Give the Partisans a little more time and no doubt Marion would soon show up.

The Partisan underground network was amazing! We sadly related the news about Howard, our bombardier, and Kuch, both of whom had been left behind in one of the villages. No matter what our privations and hardships, this was better than lying injured and in pain with an unknown future. One of the two airmen to join our group was Sam Schnear, waist gunner on Adams' plane. Schnear, Gordon, and three others were flying with Adams for the first time on the Udine mission.

The rain was coming down steadily. The Partisans kept up the pace, striking off into the black of night on narrow paths that led continually upward. The mountain was heavily wooded, but the trail offered little protection from the rain. We slipped on the muddy path, swearing as we plodded on.

Peering into the darkness we could see only gray sheets of rain. Thoroughly soaked, the odor of our sheepskin-lined jackets became oppressive, and the added weight was an extra burden. Stumbling over rocks in the darkness my heavy boots became a drag. The rain and coldness were tearing at my gut, seeping into my mind, paralyzing my thoughts. I forced myself to put one foot in front of the other. I heard Brown behind me muttering, "How could we be so lucky as to be blessed with this damn rain?"

Looking ahead on one of the switch backs I noticed three women at the front of the group, carrying huge piles of hides on their backs. Difficult for us to walk on the slippery path, we marveled at the women who balanced their heavy loads with expertise. The women were thin and tough. Dressed in men's clothes these Partisan women were carrying those hides to a tannery hidden in the mountains.

The path continued, winding and turning. We stumbled over fallen rock, rubbed against the mountain side, slipped dangerously close to the edge of the path. My sore knee continued to plague me. As we gained altitude the temperature fell. The rain turned to snow and the cold added to our other miseries. Accustomed to skimming through space at 150 miles an hour, we weren't used to traveling by foot, one torturous mile after another. Conversation had slowed to only a grunt, a smile, a wave of the arm. When we finally reached the top of the mountain the guides entered a small stone hut. Inside were Partisans sleeping on benches, and a fire was burning in the middle of the dirt floor. With only a small opening in the ceiling the walls were black with soot and the smoky haze made breathing difficult.

The Partisans were dressed in a strange assortment of civilian clothes and captured enemy uniforms. The red stars on their bill caps were the only item common to all of them. Highly disciplined, they were young and devoted to Tito and the Partisan cause. Several girls offered us soup from the huge iron pot hanging from a chain above the fire. Hungry as we were, the watery concoction looked horrible and we swallowed only a few mouthfuls to warm us.

Adjoining the small room was a larger one covered with a canvas top. There a fire burned brightly. This isolated mountain hut seemed to be a headquarters for the Partisans in the area. We took off our soggy flight jackets to dry, drew close to the fire, and reached out with our arms to absorb its warmth. Never had a fire and shelter been more welcome.

The guides and women with the heavy back packs had patiently endured the rain and long climb without complaint. Celebrating the warmth of the fire, they joined the other Partisans in spirited singing, filling the tent-top with their rousing songs, merrymaking, and laughter. Their bright and hopeful faces warmed our hearts. Surely we could trust these courageous people to return us to safety.

As warmth permeated our bodies, we lay down and slept. Rest was short lived, however, for in two hours we were boldly awakened by our hosts who poked us and indicated it was time to be moving. Stiff and sore we were scarcely able to move. How could these Partisans withstand the hardships and still have the stamina to walk miles in mountain terrain with so little rest?

Our clothes were partially dry and we were in a better position to face the strong wind and blowing snow. The Partisans in the hut joined the women and our guides as we started down the mountain. Now with a larger party, silence was imperative. After slipping down the murderous mud paths for at least half an hour the guides stalled. After a short wait we continued on until we reached a cliff. Beyond, we were told was the Adriatic Sea.

The biting wind tore through our clothing. We waited in the freezing cold, seeking refuge from the wind by standing close together. We realized walking and moving would be our only salvation in this bitter weather, and the guides would soon decide which route to take. The scouts patrolling the area returned and brought bad news. German sentries were near. The guides reversed our route and we began climbing back up the brutal trail we had come down only a short time ago.

These were the worst hours of the night. Fatigue, the pain in my knee, and the cold reduced me to a semi-conscious condition. Time stopped. We went on and on, always in the same place, always in the same swirling snow.

Reaching an area protected from the wind and snow, we came to a halt and waited, huddling together and harboring the little warmth our bodies could generate. The Partisans dared not light a fire for fear of being detected. Numb with cold we waited in a kind of shivering nightmare.

House in Kosi, Croatia where the allied airmen hid behind a false wall that sealed off the cellar behind the rock foundation.

DAY FOUR • TUESDAY • MARCH 21

The snow had stopped by the time the guides gave the command to start walking. As the mist and clouds lifted, we looked back at the cliffs rising behind us. It gave me the cold chills to see those treacherous mountains we had crossed in the night. One misstep on the rocky ledges could have meant death. Morning light lifted our spirits and the trail didn't seem so foreboding. At some other time, we would have appreciated the beauty of our surroundings. Tall pines cloaked with snow, covered the rugged mountains. Growing up in the prairies of Iowa I was awe-struck by the grandeur.

Our guides set a faster pace and we struggled to keep up. Wet snow clung to our heavy boots, making each step a burden. We climbed over fallen trees, crawled up steep inclines, grabbed hold of tree roots or branches. Each hill looked like the last one. In our weariness we asked, "How much longer?"

"Samo cez ta breg," was their reply or "Just over the next hill." This phrase became the Partisans' theme song.

At the top of a high cliff we saw a clearing where trees had been sheared as if hit by a tornado. Looking around we found pieces of a B-17 scattered over a wide area. We wondered if parts of our plane were resting on a similar mountainside. Reaching a high peak, we could see range after range of mountains. We were grateful for the protection of trees and rough terrain and marveled at the sense of direction shown by our young guides. The mountains belonged to the Partisans, not the Germans. Stopping to rest we slumped down on fallen logs, aching in every limb. My knee was throbbing with pain. Limping over to Spoon I asked, "How's it going?"

"The head's pretty good but my damn feet are driving me crazy." Spoon's flying boots, designed to cover his electric sock-like shoes, had never been intended for much walking. I slipped the half loaf of black bread out of my pocket. Was it only yesterday the farmer's wife had given it to me? Noticing the guides had no food, we shared our bread with them. One of the women carrying a backpack of hides passed around a kind of jelly, not sweet but better than nothing. We were too many people for so little food.

Seeing the crashed B-17 was a sobering experience for each of us. Our narrow escape yesterday was proof we had landed in a country well controlled by the Germans. Intelligence had warned us to avoid the Ustashi Croatians who collaborated with the Axis, but we knew little about the civil war and puppet governments fighting for control. We didn't realize that German sympathizers could be found in almost every village or town.

29

Tired, hungry, and scared, we could not fully appreciate how fortunate we were to have fallen into the hands of Tito's Partisans.

We set off again in single file down a snowy track. In time we reached easier footing, taking switchbacks through heavily forested hills. I couldn't decide which was more tiring, climbing up steep paths or bracing myself on the downhill track, now slick from the partially melted snow. Again, we asked, "How much longer?" We already knew the guides' reply, "Sarno cez ta breg."

At dusk we approached a town nestled in a valley. Unaware of our position we asked the guide for information. Language problems continued to bother us but we figured we were in western Yugoslavia, not too far from Italy. This town, called Gerovo, could have been Timbuktu for all we knew, but to have reached our destination and be able to rest was cause for celebration.

With no Partisan headquarters in the town we were taken to a picturesque old building on main street which had served as a hotel before the war. Robert Howard, bombardier on Gordon's plane, bounded down the steps to greet us. Howard, or Howie as he was called, landed near Gerovo, and had been enjoying the villagers' good food and hospitality for two days. I don't know which was more welcome – finding another one of our men, eating the meal prepared by the women in the town, or discovering we would be sleeping in the town's hotel.

Gordon, Spoon, and I shared one room. It was unheated, but there was a bed. After walking for more than twenty hours, our first move was to take off our boots and socks. Our feet were swollen and covered with blisters, many open and bleeding. I recalled the times I had laughed at Mother's cure-all for healing cuts by soaking the sores in Clorox and warm water. Now I would have welcomed both the home remedy and Mother's tender care.

We amused ourselves by counting our blisters and comparing notes to see who had the most. I had the least, for my GI shoes fit well and offered good protection. Spoon's and Gordon's problem was their type of footgear. When flying missions, the temperature in the plane often reached forty or fifty degrees below zero. Some of us wore heavy sheepskin lined clothing and regular ankle-high shoes. Others had been issued electric flying suits and heavy socks made from two layers of fabric with electric wires in between. Connected to the electrical system in the plane, the light weight clothing provided warmth without constricting the movements of the wearer.

Bailing out on a few seconds notice, there was no time to change into heavier clothing, even if it had been available. Fortunately, supply had been temporarily out of electric suits so most of my men had been issued the more common sheepskin-lined jackets. Not so for boots. Both Spoon and Gordon were wearing socks with electric wires in the shape of an S. Their soles were blistered in the same shape. Because the electric socks did not fit in regulation ankle-high shoes, they were worn inside stylish flight boots — boots never intended for walking. With each step the boots rubbed up and down as the socks gradually worked down to the toe of the boot. Walking over mountainous terrain in this footgear was pure hell. Despite the blisters and the throbbing in his head from the bomb bay injury, Spoon never complained.

After two-days of tramping through the mountains in rain and snow, everyone was sore and exhausted and ready for the blessed escape of sleep.

DAY FIVE • WEDNESDAY • MARCH 22

After breakfast we told Howie the events of the last days — hiding in the cellar, and hiking for more than twenty hours in rain and snow through the mountains to reach this town. We began to talk about our parachute jump. March 18, 10:05, was a time we would never forget.

I drew closer as Curry started talking. "The way them Jerries peppered us full of holes and set our ship on fire, it's a miracle any of us got out. From the tail I could see the wing on fire. I had my chest pack on before Munsen told us to bail out. When he gave the order, it didn't take me long to get to the tail hatch. But it was jammed! When I got up to the waist hatch, I thought all you guys were gone. It was a scary feeling. Man, did I jump out of that plane in a hurry!"

"The wind kind of took my chute, and that scared me. I didn't count to ten but pulled the rip cord right away. It gave me a funny feeling to float down so slowly. I saw the Adriatic and prayed I wouldn't land there. Did you guys see them fighters following us down? I was so close I could see the pilot in his cockpit. He made a wide circle around us but didn't bother me."

"Luckily a tree broke my fall. I landed about eight feet above the ground. My harness and chute were a mess, all tangled in the branches. By twisting and unraveling the cords I finally got free and climbed down. There was a little snow and it was cold. I walked around for hours without seeing a soul. I'd seen so many chutes when I was in the air, I figured we'd all be together on the ground. I was scared. It seemed I'd landed on another planet."

"Then I saw two guys with blue caps and red stars. Gosh, did I feel better then! They took me to a camp where there were five more men and a gal. We stayed all night in a little hut. Six of them guys and I slept in a big, long bed. The Partisan gal slept in the middle. The next day they took me to a cabin where I saw Lieutenant Williamson and Sully. Gee, I'm glad I'm here!"

I grinned. "Even after that miserable hike in the rain and cold?" Down deep we were all grateful to be alive. Now if only Marion would show up.

Howie was near the door talking to an old man who had just come in. They walked over to our table and Howie introduced him. His name was Turk, but we soon nicknamed him "The Interpreter." He had lived in the United States and learned English while working in Kansas. When he had saved enough money, he moved back to his home town. Now, able to translate for us, the old man was the VIP of Gerovo.

Relieved to have someone who could speak our language, we learned from "The Interpreter" we would stay in his village at least a day. Stiff and sore, we were glad for the chance to sleep, eat, and rest our feet. Lucky for us, Gerovo had a good supply of flour. Several women made hot rolls, a treat after eating the dry brown bread with straw filler. The beverage they called coffee was another story. It had a bitter taste and I could hardly finish one cup. We learned from Turk it was made from ground, roasted grain. At least it was hot. While we were eating, I overheard Williamson telling about his jump.

"I didn't open my parachute right away. Oddly enough I had no sensation of falling. The air was going by me as if I were standing in a wind tunnel. When I finally pulled the ripcord, I found myself upside down. Then the chute blossomed and opened, and I felt like I was jerked back upwards. The sound of air rushing by me had lost its roar."

"When I landed, I hid my parachute. There were patches of snow on the ground. I walked up the mountain. I had no gun and no compass. A little girl came up to me. She had seen my parachute and she said, 'Deutsch?' I said, 'Americana — no comprende.' She took me to her village and there I met Curry and Sully. I bargained with the woman of the house. By showing her where my parachute was hidden, she let me sleep in a bed."

While we were talking, several of the fellows had gone outside to look around the village and we joined them. Turk and Howie led us to the cemetery. A few days earlier the villagers had buried nine of our airmen who had died in the crash of the plane we saw in the mountains. Each grave was decorated with a small American flag, made with scraps of colored paper. We bowed our heads and gave tribute to these men who had given their lives for our cause. We asked Turk to express our gratitude to his people for giving our men a burial service.

In the evening the villagers celebrated our safe arrival by holding a dance in the town hall. Most of the young men were fighting in Tito's army, so the girls took advantage of having some handsome American airmen as dancing partners. Blisters don't heal in a day, so Gordon, Spoon and I decided to stay in our room and catch up on sleep.

Reiss told us later, "An old fellow played polkas on a squeeze box. I can't dance worth a tinker's damn, but I didn't have a choice. This big babe came up, grabbed me, and pulled me out on the floor."

We had noticed that our guides wore boots with cleats on the soles. Helpful on mountain trails, they could be a problem on the dance floor — at least for the partner. The girls, many of them Partisans, also wore these boots. Thinking he could dance better in his stocking feet, Reiss had taken off his prize English boots. "This babe," he said, "was whirling me around and stomped on my foot with them killer boots. I yelped with pain. She must have thought it funny, for she stomped on me again. No more dancing for me with those Yugoslav dames."

Partisans approaching a cabin in Yugoslavia - 1944

DAY SIX • THURSDAY • MARCH 23

After eating black bread with coffee, the Catholics in our group went to mass in the village church. Conducted in Latin by the local priest, the service was the same as those Reiss had attended at home. Coming out of the church Reiss had tears in his eyes. "Here we are, thousands of miles from home, and they've got the same mass as we have at home."

"Did you go to confession?" Brown asked.

"Sure thing, but the priest didn't understand a word I said." "That's the kind of confession to have!" Brown joked.

"All kidding aside, it sure makes me feel better to go to mass. My mother seemed real close, the Virgin Mary, too. Our prayers are gonna bring us home safe."

After hearing Reiss tell about the beauty of the small church, we walked over to see it. Simple in design from the outside, the interior contained beautiful mosaics depicting Christ and the Virgin Mary. The altar and carved baptismal font were overlaid with gold. In the quiet serenity of the sanctuary I thanked God for the Partisans and Yugoslavs who had helped us and prayed that we would soon reach Italy. After saying the Lord's Prayer, I was filled with peace.

Leaving the church, we met a number of men and young boys carrying guns and other usable parts from the wrecked plane we had seen in the mountains. In his broken English, Turk explained that stripping fallen Allied planes was one source of guns and equipment. Another was confiscating rifles and ammunition from the enemy. The Partisans' army was neither well equipped nor well uniformed, but what they lacked in material things they made up for in daring, discipline, and dedication to their cause.

Late in the afternoon the Partisans brought in another airman, a navigator with the 97th Bomb Group. He limped into the hotel and told us his story.

"Target was the airdrome at Udine. As we turned west and south and were approaching the IP, a swarm of Focke-Wulfs hit us. All of a sudden, I was thrown violently around and heard a loud ripping noise. Our right wing suffered a direct hit. As I picked myself up and started for the escape hatch, I heard the order to bail out. Mac, our bombardier was right behind me. I opened the door and was thrown out. When my parachute opened, I saw our ship spiraling to the ground. Both tail and wing were completely severed. God, it was awful! The others didn't have a chance."

DAY SEVEN • FRIDAY • MARCH 24

Two days of rest in Gerovo had been a godsend, both physically and emotionally. Raw blisters on Gordon's and Spoon's feet needed attention. Two women found clean rags to cover the men's sores, but rest was the best medicine. The food and shelter given by the villagers had lifted our spirits.

Turk thought we should stay in the safety of the mountains another day, but the Partisans decided it was time for us to move. About ten in the morning we saw horses pull two wooden wagons, about the size of pony carts, through the main street of the village. Our group of 13 airmen, Turk, and a new guide squeezed into these small kolas with the drivers. Crowded, we were grateful for the chance to ride. When we questioned Turk about his partner, he explained this man was chosen to make contact with the Partisan headquarters in the next large town. Turk would be going with us only part way. Changing guides was common practice among the Partisans. The first guides knew the route from town A to B, the second from town B to C, and so on. No one person would accompany us throughout our entire trek.

Leaving Gerovo, the narrow road twisted and turned, taking a downhill route. As the kolas rumbled along, we bumped over fallen rock, pitched and jolted along at a slow pace. We were in a jovial mood. Turk and the guide were amused by our antics. One of the fellows started singing, "Happy Days are Here Again." Everyone joined in and one song led to another. The driver took a mouth organ out of his hip pocket, put it to his lips and played a few tunes. The Croatians had a way of enjoying the simple pleasures of life.

After following the river, we reached a broad valley and saw farmers plowing their fields with horses. Plum trees bordered the river. Peace and serenity surrounded us.

We rode through villages where farmers' cottages clustered together on either side of the single road. We were an odd sight, with wagons hauling men, not hay, and soldiers singing at the top of their voices. Small groups of villagers lined the street and stared at this group of strangers in unfamiliar uniforms. Children peeked from behind their mothers' skirts as the women felt our sheepskin-lined jackets and admired our watches. Usually one or two old men talked to us in broken English. Like Turk, they had worked years ago in the United States in the coal mines or steel mills, returning to retire in their home village.

The horses had been watered and fed, but we were starved. After midday the drivers pointed to a group of houses in the distance. As we clattered into the little hamlet, we were greeted by smiles and shouts of "Zdiravos!" Couriers must have preceded us, for the women had prepared a generous meal of stew containing real meat, good bread, and the usual rakija. We wouldn't forget the name of this town, Turki, and the generosity of the people.

The winter of 1944 was unusually cold. In addition to suffering heavy casualties while fighting the Germans, the Partisans suffered severely from lack of food and clothing. We constantly thought or dreamed about food. We never got enough. At the same time, we knew the women were giving food they desperately needed for their families.

While eating we met an attractive dark-haired girl, tall and well-built, wearing a German tunic, black breeches and boots, all won in combat. About 21 years of age, her rank in the Partisan army was equivalent to our first lieutenant. When she moved to grasp the pistol hanging from her belt, we noticed both the index and second fingers on her right hand were missing. For two years, Turk told us, she had hidden in the woods, tramped the hills, been bombed and machine-gunned and, in turn, had killed many Germans.

After dinner we toured the town. We found a barber shop and a small building fitted out as a first aid clinic. Without bathing or shaving for a week, the grimy stubble on our faces was itchy and uncomfortable. Brown and I were first in line for a shave, glad for the money in our escape kits which allowed us this luxury.

We were surprised to find medical services in the town. Many Partisans soldiers were being treated for frost bite. Nurses changed bandages for our men who had open blisters or wounds. As new bandages and medicines were applied to Gordon's and Spoon's feet, the soiled cloths were saved. Medical supplies were scarce, and bandages were washed over and over until they were threadbare.

Reiss and Curry stood by as a doctor checked the wound in Spoon's head. "Take a look," bragged Spoon. "See them brains? You guys are always cussing me out about not having any brains."

"Sure, Spoon. We see 'em. Must be special for they're blue."

The lining of his cap had stained his wound blue. Both Reiss and Curry turned away as the doctor cleaned the gash in Spoon's scalp. We were amazed that Spoon never complained. The doctor covered the wound with a freshly washed bandage, but by the time we left town Spoon was sporting his Daniel Boone cap again.

When we mentioned our surprise about available medical aid, Turk told us this small hospital was one of a network established by the Partisans. A larger one, he said, was in Kocevski Rog about twenty miles from the town. Constructed in the mountains and at the end of a winding forest path, the site was cleverly camouflaged for protection against the Germans, Ustashi and Chetniks. The approach was blocked at intervals by barriers of logs and brushwood. Sentinels were posted throughout the area. Even the wounded were led or carried blindfolded along the secret trails leading to the hospital. Care of the Partisan wounded was an important commitment made by Tito and his staff.

With bandaged feet and full stomachs, we climbed into the kolas. Our morale had increased one hundred percent. The villagers seemed equally enthusiastic about seeing American airmen who were helping their cause. The people stood by the side of the road, saluting with clenched fists and yelling, "Zivio Arnericani!" and "Zivio Tito!"

The road twisted and turned, following the Kupa River. Snow-peaked mountains framed plowed fields bordering the river. Cramped as we were, we took catnaps while bumping along the rough road. Then it started to snow. My feet and hands were freezing. We understood why so many Partisans were being treated for frostbite.

In the evening we entered Brod na Kupi. It was devastated. Only smoke-scarred walls and piles of rubble were the sorry remains. No shelter for Partisans or Americans in this place. Turk told us the Ustashi had burned the town. Although warned about the Ustashi in briefings, we hadn't realized the extent of the political turmoil and warring factions in Yugoslavia. Brod na Kupi was at the intersection of two main roads. Essential for military communication, telephone service to other communities had been restored by the Partisans. An earlier call had relayed our need for transportation.

Turk prepared to return to Gerovo with the horse-drawn kolas. He told us we would find a large Partisan headquarters in the next town and American liaison officers would meet us. Though we were eager to be on our way, Turk's services as translator had been invaluable and we were sorry to see him go. Saying good-bye, he handed me several letters to mail when we returned to the United States.

An old Italian truck pulled up to the kolas. We piled into the back, crowding close together. The battered truck was one of the spoils of war following the capitulation of the Italian army. The driver had been an Italian soldier who changed loyalties and stayed to fight with the Partisans. He accepted his duties as a truck driver with peculiar zeal. With great gusto he shot around hairpin turns, alternately speeding and slamming on the brakes, throwing us from one side to the other. Above the growl of the engine we heard his fine tenor voice singing Grand Opera in Italian with the same passion he gave to his driving. Maneuvering the vehicle at reckless speeds, the driver evidently placed no value on his life, nor ours. We were all jittery. Even walking would be better than riding with a maniac.

Reaching our destination, the driver took us to the Partisan headquarters, an old building at the edge of town. Climbing out of the truck I gave thanks we had arrived safely.

With the customary clenched fist, our guide greeted the Kommandant Mesta. "Zdravo!"

"Zivio Tito," replied the Kommandant. I noticed a large pot in the corner of the room and was glad when our guide motioned for us to eat. How many times that bone had been cooked and re-cooked I couldn't say. At least the soup was hot. New faces appeared. Gordon, Schnear and Howie jumped up to greet their pilot, Edward J. Adams, and navigator, Edward Doran.

Adams greeted Gordon. "Where in the hell have you been? Doran and I've been here for days, enjoying the good life."

"We're damn ready to sample some of that easy living," said Gordon. "We've tramped through hell and just escaped sudden death at the hands of a maniac Italian driver."

Everyone started talking at once. We never tired of recounting the details of bailing out of our plane, the first and only such experience for most of us. Adams described his jump.

"After giving the order to bail out, I heard someone call from the nose section that there was trouble getting the escape hatch open. I climbed down, and between the three of us we managed to force the door open. After tumbling out of the plane, I looked down and the Adriatic seemed awfully close. I was worried about being blown over the water. My problems would have been over in a few minutes had I landed in frigid water with my heavy winter clothing. Fortunately, the wind was from the west which moved me inland.

"I landed on a rocky slope near a wooded area. I could hear German voices calling as the soldiers searched for us. I decided my best chance was to stay put until dark. I crouched under a fallen log until I heard the voices fade in the distance. Then I found a better place to hide and waited until nightfall. I walked most of the night. The next day I saw a teenage girl working in a field. She contacted the Partisans. Doran joined me four days ago."

Doran explained he and Adams had been treated like kings. They stayed with a family, had good food and comfortable beds. They could visit in English with the father who had worked in Chicago until the early thirties.

Doran had landed on a mountain ridge in three feet of snow. Looking down he could see the Adriatic shore. "Below me I could see men moving and firing weapons. I hid my chute and tore up any target information in my small notebook. After walking east for about five hours I met a thirteen-year-old boy. He took me to the Partisans and they brought me to Delnice."

Doran told us it was a town of several thousand people. A ski lift had attracted tourists to this mountainous area before the war began. Delnice was chosen as the headquarters for the Communist Party in this part of Croatia and many of the townspeople were loyal to the Partisans.

"Have you had any idea where we are, or where we are going?" I asked Adams. Neither he nor Doran were sure of our exact position. We knew we were near the coast since many of us had seen the Adriatic when we bailed out. Like us, they hoped we would soon make contact with a boat to take us across the Adriatic to Bari.

We questioned Adams about the American liaison officers Turk told us would be at the Partisan headquarters in Delnice. He had seen neither American nor British officers. For now, all we could do was trust the Partisans to get us to Italy safely.

The people in Delnice welcomed us with open arms. Spoon, Gordon, Seward, and I were taken to a two-story house where a woman lived with her two daughters. We were offered the upstairs guest room where we slept under clean white sheets and blankets. The woman pampered us as if we were her sons and we loved it.

DAY EIGHT • SATURDAY • MARCH 25

When we were awakened it was almost noon. Downstairs, Maria, the twenty-year-old daughter of Gospodja Volf, greeted us. No schools were open in the town, so Maria had been teaching her little sister to read. She cleared the books from the table and set it for dinner. The kitchen window framed a view of the mountains. Always hungry, we ate our meal with gusto. The soup, rich with barley and a little meat, was delicious and even the coarse brown bread tasted good.

Eager to check on other members of the crew, we walked to the Partisan headquarters. Seven days ago, we bailed out over this Balkan country, and now we were no closer to leaving than when we landed. But we were in a safer location and protected by people sympathetic to the Partisan cause.

Entering the Partisan headquarters, Sully approached me. "Got a cigarette?"

Reiss added, "Pop, here, has been trying to bum a smoke off every sucker who walks in."

I wanted to help Sully, but the cigarettes in my escape kit had gone to our Partisan guides. American cigarettes were highly prized in Yugoslavia and would buy almost anything, except freedom. Sully had used Reiss's ration days ago. We would always be hungry, but for smokers like Sully, being deprived of cigarettes was a greater hardship than having too little food. The Kommandant Mesta called me over to the table at the far end of the room. He peppered me with questions. When were we shot down? Where? How many got out? What group were we with? Again, we gave our names, serial numbers and home addresses for the Partisan records.

The fellows were chewing the fat about when and how we might return to Bari, but there was not even a rumor to give us hope. The main news was about a dance to be held that night at the community building. We found dancing a popular entertainment among the Yugoslavs. While Gordon and Spoon looked for the local hospital unit to have their bandages changed, I went back to our room for a little sack time. A real bed with sheets was a luxury.

Everyone attended the dance. Gordon and Spoon each vied for the opportunity to escort Maria, but Gordon's bars won out. With dark hair and fair complexion, Maria was stunning in a black skirt and sweater and black calf-length boots. Maria couldn't speak English, but who needs to talk when holding a pretty girl close.

Before the dance, a speech was delivered by a high-ranking officer in the Partisan army. He was interrupted frequently with cheers from the audience: "Smrt Fasizmu!" "Sloboda Narovu!" and "Zivio Tito!" There was much clapping and stamping of feet as the people cried, "Death to Fascism, Freedom to the People and Long Live Tito."

The sound of Slovenian folk tunes, played on concertinas by a couple of older men, brought the Yugoslavs out on the dance floor. As in our square dances, the dancers formed a circle and repeated traditional steps. Loud cheers followed the verses claiming Stalin and Tito's victories. The dance floor became crowded when the musicians played waltzes in a slower tempo. When I saw Brown dancing with Maria, I knew Gordon's and Spoon's feet were more painful than they had let on.

I worked my way around the outer edge of the room, anxious to meet other Allied airmen. Harding, a tail gunner, explained that he was one of twelve who had landed in Southern Austria. Like us, they had reached Delnice with the assistance of the Partisans. Harding introduced me to two Englishmen from South Africa; one of them was named George. A linguist, he spoke Italian fluently and had picked up the Slavic language as well. Captured in November 1941 in North Africa, George and his friend had been held prisoners of war in northern Italy. When Mussolini surrendered to the Allies in September of 1943, they escaped from their POW camp, hid in the mountains, and gradually worked their way east to Yugoslavia. George was especially concerned about his mother, for he had not been able to write her for more than a year. Many of us wondered how long it would be before our parents would know we were alive.

Now our little group of 13 had expanded to 25 and each had a personal adventure to share.

DAY NINE • SUNDAY • MARCH 26

After breakfast Maria, her mother, and sister prepared to attend Mass. In each town or village, we were in, we noticed the people were religious and took pride in their church, usually Roman Catholic. Reiss, and others who were Catholic, attended Mass with the townspeople.

Leaving Gordon and Spoon at the house nursing their feet, Seward and I walked around the town. We met Brown, Sully and Curry and talked about the guys back at the base. With blue skies overhead, we wondered where the 97th would be flying.

"The guys will be at 'em today," Sully said.

Brown was concentrating on something. "Do you hear planes, or is it my imagination?"

We squinted and searched the skies for any sign of activity. We could see nothing but heard a low hum in the distance. Planes must be up there some place.

"Suppose it's the damn Germans," muttered Sully.

"I doubt it," I said. "Sounds like a hell of a group."

After a few minutes Curry pointed his finger toward the west. "Them are bombers all right — our bombers." Finally, we all spotted them at three o'clock. The formation from the ground was impressive — wave after wave of Fortresses and Liberators glittering in the sunshine with fighters diving and weaving on the fringes.

"What's the target? Udine again?"

"Don't know, but it could be Fiume," said Brown. "I saw the airdrome from my parachute. In any case, plenty of Germans around there."[4]

Curry added thoughtfully, "Wish I was with 'em. I'd rather be up there taking my chances than down here."

I agreed with Curry. "I'm going to miss the flying. Being down here finishes it for us. Our days of bombing the Jerries are over." We all knew the rule that men were not permitted to fly into a theater of war where they had evaded or escaped capture.

---

[4] Target for Fifteenth Air Force B-17 groups was the aircraft component plant in Steyr, Austria. Bad weather forced them to strike the secondary target: docks and shipping ports in Fiume.

"I could do with some of them doughnuts the Red Cross girls gave us when we came back from a mission," said Curry.

"And the whiskey," said Seward. "Don't forget the whiskey."

In the afternoon we attended a meeting for evadees held at the local Communist headquarters. A large picture of Stalin hung on one wall. Townspeople crowded into the small room, eager to hear news of family members fighting with the Partisans.

The Kommandant Mesta started his speech with the usual Communist Party declarations: "Smrt Fasizmu!" and "Sloboda Narovu!" someone shouted, "Zivio Marshall Tito." The crowd repeated the salute to their popular leader. Another voice called out, "Zivio Marshall Stalin!" The rafters rang with shouts of "Zivio Marshal Stalin!" Although there were no tributes to Churchill or Roosevelt, the Partisans showed their commitment by protecting us and other airmen. Their personal sacrifices showed their gratitude for the supplies and ammunition parachuted by Allied pilots to Partisan forces.

For us the Kommandant's speech was a jumble of gibberish. As we were not able to understand a word he said, George, the Englishman from South Africa, translated the main part of the message that concerned us.

"In two or three days the Partisan guides will take us through the German lines to the Adriatic coast. There, a boat will be waiting to carry us across the sea to Bari. After landing in Italy, the Americans will take care of us. The Kommandant says the worst part of the trip is over."

Now it was our turn to cheer. In a few days we would be back at our base in Amendola — safe from the dangers and privations in this German occupied Balkan country.

DAY TEN • MONDAY • MARCH 27

We woke up to snow on Monday morning. A storm had moved in during the night and a thick, white carpet covered the gray landscape. I recalled the ski lift on the outskirts of town. Though great for skiing, this was not good weather for walking long distances on mountain trails blanketed with a foot of snow.

I had slept well. Offered a bed with sheets and blankets, I had been able to sleep for the first time without wearing my heavy outer clothes. As I put on my jacket I thought of my return to Italy. Only two or three more days the Kommandant had said. Even the snow-packed mountain trails seemed insignificant now.

When we arrived at the Partisan headquarters, we saw two kolas with horses parked in front of the building. As Gordon and Spoon hobbled behind me, I realized these wagons were furnished for the men with bandaged feet. Here again, the people in Delnice showed their generous hospitality with good food, comfortable beds and kolas. We were a large group now — twenty-five airmen joking and bantering in the cold, winter air. Four Partisans waited to guide us on this the final leg of our journey. They were young with red stars stitched to their caps and wearing the usual strange assortment of civilian clothes and captured uniforms.

The snow had let up, but the low-lying clouds obscured our view of the mountains. As the trail led upwards, we knew we had reached the foothills of the majestic peaks admired yesterday. Kicking the wet snow from our boots, we hurried to keep pace with the horses. Spoon's coonskin cap made him conspicuous among the other riders. He waved at us and kept up a constant chatter, punctuated with cuss words.

Following the wagons on the winding road we started singing "Lili Marlene," the song we borrowed from the Germans as our national overseas song. Our spirits were not dampened by the weather, lack of food, or the rocky road. March can go out like a lion in Yugoslavia as well as back home, I thought. Today's snow and bitter north wind were a bleak contrast to yesterday's clear skies and soft weather. I turned up my collar and plodded on.

The valley narrowed, and we were headed directly for the mountains. If there was a choice of roads, we soon learned ours would be the higher, steeper trail. Again, "over the next hill" came to be our common refrain. After several hours of struggling up the rugged path we saw sheepherders coming toward us, driving their little flocks.

We moved aside to let them pass, dragging our feet through the new fallen snow. Some of the hamlets we passed were no more than a cluster of a few stone cottages. People peered out of their low doorways and stared at the long column of soldiers tramping through their valley.

By mid-afternoon we reached the small town of Mrkopolj, about 20 miles as the crow flies from the Adriatic. We heard the laughter of children as they fired snowballs from behind snow forts. Even the young were playing war.

We were divided into small groups and families in the town took us into their homes. Gordon, Spoon, Seward, and I stayed with a poor woman whose husband was fighting with the Partisans. She lived with her young son in a hut made of mud and plaster with a thatched roof. Furnishings were few, but the house was clean. Food supplies from last fall's harvest were almost depleted, so there was little to share with four hungry young men. Potatoes boiled in plenty of water with no salt were made into a thin soup and served in a large wooden bowl placed in the center of the table. Each of us had a spoon and helped ourselves from a common bowl. An old cow, sheltered in the lean-to, provided a little milk for the child. Our bed was tile floor with a cover of straw.

Many people in Yugoslavia lived in true poverty, but time and again thee reached out to us, strangers in their land, and shared the little they had.

DAY ELEVEN • TUESDAY • MARCH 28

I awoke to the clattering of lids on the iron stove. The room was icy cold. I saw the woman pushing sticks of wood into the fire box. I got up to help. It would be warmer moving around than lying on the cold floor.

Breakfast consisted of the same watery potato soup, warmed over from last night. The thin, frail son finished his soup quickly, looking for more. We too, were hungry, but it was the growing boy who needed our food. He watched our every move. Gordon put him on his knee, grinning as the boy touched his flight helmet and caressed the soft leather of his flight jacket. We tried to thank the woman who had shared one of her most valuable possessions, food. As we left, the boy stood outside the door and waved.

By mid-morning the fellows had crowded into the one small bar in town. We all had script money from our escape kits, but a glass of bitter schnapps was the only choice. Soon a couple of Partisans came in and told us it was time to go.

Outside the bar we found several new guides placing bridles on the two horses, each harnessed to a kola. The wheels on the small wagons had been fitted with wooden runners. Except for their smaller size they reminded me of the farm wagons, with runners, used for sleigh rides at home. Again, the fellows with injuries and bandaged feet would ride in style. The rest of us started walking in front of the horse-drawn kolas for obvious reasons. A mild, bitter wind whipped our faces and tore through our clothes as we headed for the mountain trails.

The trail twisted and turned as we climbed higher and higher, slipping and sliding on the snow-covered rocky path. Caked with wet snow, our boots became heavier and heavier. About once every hour the guides gave a signal to halt. As the word was passed down the line each of us made a dash for the closest rock or log.

Brown, Reiss and I had found places near one another when Brown caught my attention. "Look behind you. Old Whiney is at it again, trying to climb into one of the wagons."

'Give Spoon and Gordon time. They'll handle Whiney," I said.

Brown looked up. "Damn rotten conduct for an officer — or for anyone. He's an embarrassment."

Reiss also had noticed Whiney trying to squeeze in among the injured.

"Throw the son-of-a-bitch out, Spoon."

"Whiney has threatened over and over to quit," said Brown. "Wish somebody'd call his bluff."

Spoon cussed as he pushed the young officer over the side of the kola. Picking himself up and brushing the snow off his pants, Whiney reprimanded Spoon for talking back to an officer. Whiney had made a practice of pulling his rank on the lower echelon. With his constant bickering and cocky attitude, he had alienated himself from our group and the Partisans as well. We were all coping with a tough situation; reason demanded we accept our fate.

After hours of steady climbing and marching through thick woods we emerged onto a rocky precipice, with cliffs on one side and a drop on the other. The trail was steep and zigzagged sharply. It was no longer safe to ride in the kolas, so the fellows climbed out to join us. Walking was still painful for Spoon and Gordon. Their cloth electric footgear had worn out long ago. The large, outer boots, which fit over the heated ones, provided no support for the feet. When forced to walk, the men shuffled along.

The boys with flight boots had no corner on sore feet. After ten days of walking with no chance to wash clothes, our socks had big holes. The constant rubbing of skin against army shoes was painful, but the good news was we were near the Adriatic and our ordeal would soon be over.

As we climbed to higher altitudes, there were fewer trees to protect us from the biting wind and blowing snow. Our feet and hands were numb with cold. We were climbing, always climbing; the cold wind blew constantly. Finally, we reached level ground and the word to halt was passed down the line. We slumped to the ground.

Bringing up the rear were two Partisans, leading the horses pulling the empty kolas. Spoon took off his coonskin cap and bowed. We cheered as he and the others climbed into their "chariots." It was easy to envy the fellows who could ride, but none of us would trade our ability to walk for their ill-fitting boots and raw sores. As I stepped aside for the kolas to pass Spoon held his right hand high, making the "V" for victory sign and grinned, "Oh, how I grieve for you slobs who have to walk."

We had reached a plateau. Mountains loomed on either side, but the terrain ahead was fairly flat. Surely now we were "over the last hill" and headed for the Adriatic. We marched with quicker step over the *polje*. The Partisans started singing, first marching tunes — then patriotic songs saluting Stalin and Tito. We sensed the love of freedom and independence expressed in their singing.

We were in a constant state of awe at the energy expended by our guides. They could hike in the mountains for 24 hours without food and little water, seeming to have legs of iron and the stamina of an ox. The Partisans had little with which to conduct a war. Poor foot gear, no socks, no overcoats, little ammunition, obsolete guns, and no pistols except captured ones. Still their spirit and enthusiasm in fighting for freedom were unequaled.

Night had come and now it was impossible to discern the vast bulk of the mountains, but we could feel their presence. I stumbled and fell, cursing the slippery rocks, the black night. Brown reached out and offered me a hand. We were numb with cold, weary, starved for food.

As the guides slowed the pace, we smelled burnt wood and flesh. In the darkness we barely made out the ghostlike structures that had once been houses. George told us German planes had bombed and strafed scores of towns in northern Yugoslavia, dropping incendiary bombs. This town, Dresnika, had also been a victim of German reprisals. Was it because of partisan resistance or were the Germans looking for us and bombing innocent people who offered us protection?

We followed our guides through the burned town to a small building at the far edge. Amazingly the Partisan headquarters had escaped the bombing. Crowding into the small shelter the men gathered around an old woman, ladling potato soup into wooden bowls from a large iron pot. Would there be any left by the time I worked my way to the far end of the room?

Some of the fellows huddled on the floor of the headquarters building. Eight of us were taken to a small hut where we dropped, exhausted. A cold wind whistled through the cracks in the door and windows and the floor was drafty. Not even hay for cover. Wet and freezing from our nine-hour trek, sleep would not come. We got up and stood around the fire, making bets on the number of hours before reaching the coast. Escape by boat was almost within our grasp.

Bob Brown's diary with names of towns and chronological events

DAY TWELVE • WEDNESDAY • MARCH 29

A grimy but jubilant group gathered at the headquarters' building. Our guides saluted the officer in charge of the Partisan unit that would take us on the last leg of our journey. Instead of the usual two or three guides we counted ten men and two women. It was customary to see women working alongside the men. Dressed in ski trousers and woolen shirts, they carried packs on their backs and a cluster of stick grenades, fastened to their belts. With rifles slung over their shoulders, the women differed from their male counterparts mainly by the kerchiefs worn over their heads.

The day was clear and cold. I had a spectacular view of the mountain range we had walked through yesterday. The trail twisted through dense woods, going down hill more than up. Thick puffs of snow capped the long needles of evergreen. I wished Williamson had his camera. No horses or carts were permitted on this part of the trip, for we were near an area heavily occupied by the Germans and Ustashi.

By noon we reached a little valley with a few scattered houses. There were about 35 airmen and Partisans, a large number for the people in this village to feed. Bowls filled with hot *polenta* warmed us and even the coarse dry bread was welcome. Food was always on our minds and we never got enough.

The Partisan leader gave instructions in Slavic tongue. Translating, George told us we had reached the jumping off place for crossing the main road. A boat was waiting at the coast to take us to Italy. Needing the protection of darkness, we had several hours before we could move on.

When it got dark, we left the security of the little village. About a dozen more Partisans had joined our group. All were heavily armed with rifles slung over their shoulders and hand grenades fastened to their belts. The men brought two mules carrying small cannons on their backs. We fell in line behind the soldiers and mules, walking single file, six paces apart. George emphasized the importance of complete quiet. "Don't talk, and whatever you do, don't whistle," he said. "That would be a dead give-away that Allied airmen are around. The Krauts know that only Americans whistle."

Scarcely a sound was heard along the line of march. Twice challenged Partisan patrols, the guides whispered the password and went on. Cautiously, but with confidence, we followed the Partisan soldiers. These men and women did not hurry, but walked deliberately, as if they had no fear. Suddenly the long column halted. Scouts went ahead to reconnoiter. Not safe to proceed, we waited in the blackness of the night. The mules stood still and made no sound.

Standing silently, we shivered in the cold, ready to advance. Finally, the word was passed down the line and we started to move, again walking six paces apart. The road was narrow but wide enough for farmers to drive their horse-drawn *kolas* to market. We could barely see the houses and barn-like buildings on either side. Light shone through the windows of one house; we were close enough to see German soldiers sitting at a table, laughing, drinking, and playing cards.

We had passed several houses when the stillness of the night was interrupted by the sudden barking of a dog. We stopped, terrified the Germans would discover our presence. The barking stopped as suddenly as it had begun. Continuing, we passed a barn on the left side of the road. A dog lay on the ground. He wouldn't bark again.

Fearing the dog had warned the Germans, the Partisans led us off the road and back into the thick trees where they called a halt. We were a large group to be hiding in an area so heavily guarded by the enemy. The time of waiting seemed endless. Checking my watch at frequent intervals, I watched the minute hand move slowly.

Scouts left the security of the trees to check the movement of the German and Ustashi patrols. The main road below was our last hurdle. Success of the operation was dependent upon mobility and concealment. Our guides had an uncanny sense of direction in the blackness of the night, and once across the road they would lead us to the coast.

Finally, we received word to form a line and proceed. I hoped the Germans had gone back to their card playing. Approaching the highway, we saw no signs of the enemy and breathed a sigh of relief.

Suddenly bright flashes lit up the sky. Without waiting for orders, we dove down the embankment, clawed our way up the hillside and ran into the safety of the dense forest. Blasts of gunfire followed us. Panting more from fright than physical exertion, we huddled together, awaiting word from our guides. As the firing continued, the Partisans finally joined us, looking for cover from the bright flares sent skyward by the Germans.

From the wooded heights bordering the road we watched the movement of enemy soldiers walking back and forth, back and forth along the road. The Germans had posted additional soldiers for patrol. There would be no chance of crossing the road tonight.

Freedom was so close, and now so far. We had been betrayed... by a goddamn dog.

DAYS THIRTEEN TO FIFTEEN
THURSDAY THROUGH SATURDAY
MARCH 30 - APRIL 1

I slept fitfully, exhausted from the all-night march that had ended in failure to reach the coast. After tramping and groping through the tree-covered hills, we eventually reached the huts we had left the afternoon before. Now, eight or ten of us lay close together on the dirt floor of a small lean-to that usually provided shelter for the family's cow or pig. Dirty straw was our only cover, but the heat from our bodies kept us warm.

With no food since noon of yesterday we were famished. George reported that the Germans had come through, slaughtered the animals and taken most of the grain. From the people's meager food supply, we were served a warm, watery soup. The villagers evidently had no access to salt, for the soup was tasteless.

As we discussed last night's encounter with the Germans, George told us that several Partisans had been killed. Forming the advance group in our party, the Partisan soldiers had been watching the movements of the enemy and searching for the best place to cross the road. When the flares illuminated the sky, the Partisans became an easy target for the Germans. Knowing they were greatly outnumbered our guides fled to the hills. Several were killed before they could reach safety.

Again, we were amazed at the sacrifices made by the Yugoslavs. It was one thing for the villagers to share their limited food, but quite another for men to die while protecting us. Refusing to accept German rule, these people risked their lives daily in the struggle against the enemy.

The Partisans had spent the afternoon cleaning their guns. Their activity showed us we would repeat yesterday's trek — leave at sunset, walk most of the night, and once again try to cross the main road.

"Once across the German road," George said, "we will be only a short day's walk from the coast."

In the afternoon we heard gunfire in the distance. By evening a group of haggard Partisans staggered into town, looking for food. A full-scale skirmish had developed near the road we needed to cross. We realized we would be sleeping in the smelly lean-to another night.

Three days went by with no signs of leaving this godforsaken place.

Each afternoon we waited to move on. Each evening the message was the same; "Probably leave the next day." With tired soldiers joining our group the little available food had to be divided among many. A sheep had been killed, so there were a few pieces of stringy mutton in the thin soup, the only meal of the day.

We saw only a few huts in the village. One mother with a toddler and infant lived in a small one-room dwelling with a bed about the size of a cedar chest. The hut had been built in the side of the hill and the animals kept underneath. Concealed from view, her cow had escaped the German's slaughter. She was fortunate to have milk for her children.

The woman kindly offered me a dish of clabbered milk, so thick it could be eaten with a spoon. I remembered laughing at my Dad when he ate thick sour cream on bread, his favorite supper meal. But this was no laughing matter. How could I possibly swallow the sour stuff? I couldn't insult the woman, and besides, I was hungry. Somehow, I forced the sour milk down, but hungry as I was, I couldn't stomach it. I hastily retreated behind some trees where I lost it all.

We were a ragged bunch of airmen — unkempt, bearded, dirty. We had worn the same clothes, day and night, since bailing out. The only time we had seen a bar of soap was at the barber shop in Turki. After sleeping in animal quarters, lice joined the dirt and grime. As I lay down in the straw and tried to sleep, I could feel the little buggers crawling up and down my legs and arms. Exhausted, I fell asleep, but awoke before long, itching and scratching.

Waiting was more detrimental to our morale than long hours of walking. Why were we being kept in this damn hole? Standing around an open fire, the guys were arguing about when we'd get out.

"The fellows in Delnice said we'd be out in three days!"

"Hell, that's two days ago. Someone's lying. I'm putting my money on three more days."

"It's the damn dog that warned the Germans. I'm betting them guides get us across tonight."

Spoon was scratching his butt. "We'd better get out soon. The doggone lice are driving me crazy, runnin' up and down my stinkin' trunks."

"How can people live in this filth?"

"They don't. Hell, we're the ones sleeping with the lousy animals." Spoon pushed Curry away from the fire. "I'm tired of this shit. Move over, my ass is freezing."

54

"When I get back, the first thing I'm having is a hot shower."

"A hot shower at our base? You're out of your head, man! First thing I'm having is a cold beer."

We were on edge — not knowing when we would leave, nor where we would go. If we were so near the coast, why couldn't the Partisans bypass the German road? They seemed to have no plan, and time meant nothing.

It was easy for us to criticize. I thought of the young Partisans who had been killed as we attempted to cross the German road. We were lucky to be alive.

★

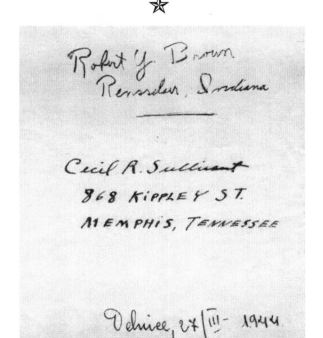

Signatures of Brown and Sullivant from their host's guest book in Delnice, 1944

DAYS SIXTEEN AND SEVENTEEN
SUNDAY & MONDAY • APRIL 2 & 3

Rumors were that this was the day to move out — rumors started, no doubt, by some of the more restless men. I wouldn't believe anything until we started walking on the trail. We were lying on the hay-covered floor of the lean-to, chewing the fat, when we heard loud cries from one of the men. Dashing outside, I saw Williamson pointing toward the sky and shouting "Planes — look at 'em! Those guys from the 97th have finally found out where we are."

As we looked up, we saw hundreds of planes, B-17's and B-24's, flying in formation high above us.

"Tell 'em to bomb the German Road, Williamson, and finish off those Jerries. Haven't you got ESP?" cried Reiss.

"I've tried contacting them, but they don't seem to pay any attention," said Williamson.

"Look at the fighters weaving in and out," said Brown. "If we'd had them on the Udine mission we'd be up there now." [5]

As the planes continued to fly east, we tried to guess their destination, suggesting probable targets. Seeing our own planes gave us a lonely feeling. In a few hours the guys would be back at the base, eating in the mess hall and sleeping on cots in our warm tents.

"Maybe Williamson's prayers will work without help from them bombers," said Curry in a hushed voice. "Maybe tonight the Partisans will get us across the German road."

Excitement filled the air. Small groups gathered, talking and gesturing, each giving an opinion as to when we would leave. We had been looking for George to find out the real scoop, and before long he walked toward us from one of the huts.

"Tonight's the night!" George shouted.

"Hell — we've heard that story every night."

---

[5] The target of this mission was the marshalling yards at Brod, Yogoslavia. On April 1st the Twelfth Air Force transferred its 31st and 52nd Fighter Groups to the Fifteenth. Pilots flying P-51s and P-47s provided the long-range escorts the Fifteenth heavy bombers needed for missions to Germany and the Balkans. The weaving fighters may have been the famous Tuskegee Airmen who were also flying out of Italy.

Putting his hand on Reiss's shoulder, George looked him straight in the eye, "Believe me, this time it's for real. I heard the Partisans talking about plans. Everything points to moving out in a few hours."

"Knock it off. I'll believe it when we're on the trail."

Evening approached, and we could see no movements among the Partisans. As the sun slid below the horizon, so did our spirits. Eight o'clock — nine o'clock — no mention of leaving. Once again, we lay down in the foul-smelling hay. Another night in the lean-to with the cow bellowing.

"Pokret!" I was awakened by the whispered command to get moving. Shivering from the cold, I got to my feet and looked at my watch. Midnight. Groaning and grumbling we stumbled out of the lean-to and joined the other men huddled outside. In spite of the cold, we came alive in the dark. George had been right after all. Hopefully this time there would be no dogs and we'd make it to the coast.

Someone mentioned food and immediately everyone rushed to the doorway of one of the huts. There stood a woman, handing each man four cold boiled potatoes. Several fellows wolfed all of theirs down at once. Some of us realized this might be our only food before reaching the coast, so we stuffed them into our pockets. As the guides pointed to the dense forest we started walking, a dark column of hopeful men relying on the Partisans to lead us to safety.

After an hour of walking we smelled the sickening odor of burned flesh. In the moonless night there was little visibility, but as the trail widened into a road we could make out the dim outline of dozens of scarred and ruined houses on either side. It reminded us of Dresnika, the town we had passed the week before. No doubt this was another village bombed by the Germans.

At the edge of town, we started climbing again; the rocky trail was slippery from those who walked ahead. Moving in the darkness in single file, I felt isolated. We had been pulled into a closed and simple world made up of trees, rocks, and mountains and before us a narrow trail that had no end. We moved as the blind, obsessed with the fear of losing touch, of being lost and left behind, alone. This was no man's land.

Finally, I heard, "Odmor." The command to stop was whispered down the line. I slumped to the ground, too exhausted to find a dead log or flat rock. Looking around to see that no one was watching, I pulled one of the cold potatoes out of my pocket and stuffed it into my mouth. Even a single potato could cause a fight among friends. I dreamed of food, — a juicy hamburger, Mother's warm apple pie, peeling an orange and eating it section by section.

My daydreaming was interrupted by the order to resume walking. The feeling of hope, even jubilation, evident when we left the village a few hours ago had turned to discontent and criticism.

"This is the same damn trail we were on a week ago."

"Yeah, that burned out village was the place we stumbled through in the dark before."

"You stumbled through? Hell, you were riding like a king in a carriage."

"Don't pay no attention to him. One stinkin' mountain is the same as all the others. Besides, it's black as hell and who knows where we are?"

"We never know where we are in this godforsaken place. Where's George? Maybe he can tell us something."

Brown and I hadn't seen George since we left the village three or four hours ago.

"What do you think?" I turned to Brown. "Are we heading for the German road?"

"George didn't say anything about where we were going — just we were leaving."

"Suppose they have another place we can get to the Adriatic without crossing that road?"

"Who knows," Bob said. "Those Partisans are mighty tight-lipped. Who can understand them anyway — except George. And I doubt he gets into their inner sanctum."

"The battered troops who came into the village were proof heavy fighting was going on. I figure the Krauts sent in extra reinforcements and after that there wasn't a chance."

"They kept us waiting long enough, sleeping and living in those lice infested stables," Bob muttered. "I'm getting damn tired of freezing to death with no food and never knowing what's goin' on."

After struggling along for another hour, we saw dawn pinking the sky and started singing. Following a single track hewn in the mountain side, we looked up at the craggy cliffs above us. For centuries these mountains had provided a refuge for the Croats from foreign invaders, and now in 1944 they were once more protecting the persecuted and oppressed, the Partisans fighting for freedom from tyranny.

In the daylight we knew we were back on the same rugged trails we had followed a week earlier. We climbed higher and higher, one hill after another. No longer bothering to ask how far to our destination, we knew the answer, "Just over the next hill." Daylight hours passed more quickly. We were always hungry and our feet ached, but most of us tried to make the most of a tough situation. Jumping across a frozen stream, Brown and I heard some yelling up ahead. "What's goin' on?"

"Several fellows are scuffling," said Gordon.

Word came down that Whiney was causing trouble again. Because of his bitching the men tried to avoid him. Once on the trail, however, someone had to walk near him and loud arguments broke out. As we approached, Whiney was seated on the ground, lashing out at anyone who came near. He had refused to walk further.

Even though he didn't deserve help, we couldn't leave anyone stranded in the mountains. George walked up, grabbed Whiney by the collar, forced him to his feet and started walking behind him. Sniveling, Whiney plodded on cursing the Partisans and anyone else within ear shot. Our plight was difficult enough without having to discipline one of our own men.

The trail reached a clearing where we looked down on a few houses huddled in a small snow-covered valley. Under different circumstances, this area could support a popular ski resort. At some other time, we too could have appreciated the lush pine forests, the spectacular snow-covered mountains peaks, but for now all we wanted were dry shoes, a comfortable bed, a good meal. Would we ever get out of this country? The fear of capture or even death took the heart out of us. Maybe we were too tough on Whiney. Not able to cope with the fear and uncertainty, he had gone off his rocker. Somehow, I had to keep faith that God was looking after me.

We dragged our feet through the heavy snow. Our bellies were empty and our backs ached. Those four little potatoes had provided scant food for a sixteen-hour hike in rugged mountain terrain. We would have given the rest of our script money for even a loaf of straw bread. Surprising how I had developed an appetite for foods I had refused two weeks ago. Hunger was almost a greater enemy than the Germans.

Overhearing the guides talk about Mrkopolj, we realized the mountain village we had left a week ago was our destination. In spite of snow and bitter winds, we had made the long trip to reach the coast in a celebrating mood; now, returning, our spirits were at low ebb. With heavy hearts we braced ourselves for the last stretch.

At dusk we climbed a high, rocky hill. From the top was a spectacular view of the valley below — tree covered hills with majestic mountain peaks rising in the distance. Below we could see a narrow, winding road leading to the village. The men cheered as Spoon raised his fingers in the "V" for victory sign. We had finally climbed the "last hill."

We were a dirty, lice-infested bunch staggering into the little town. Although disappointed and exhausted, we were thankful for the Partisan's network of trustworthy people waiting to give us food and shelter. Spoon cried out as he hobbled ahead, "This is the town with the great bar! Heads you treat me, tails I'll buy the round. See y'all!"

Letter from Dick's younger brother, Don, written on April 4, 1944

DAY EIGHTEEN • TUESDAY • APRIL 4

When we stayed overnight in Mrkopolj a week ago we had been invited into the homes of the villagers. Now our filthy clothes were infested with lice and we were only fit to sleep with the animals. Crowded together in a small barn, we needed the warmth of many bodies to keep from freezing. Every available inch of floor space was taken by some sleeping form.

In the morning, most of the fellows headed for the bar. Brown and I joined a lively, noisy group.

"I dreamt I was climbing those damn mountains and Brown here was calling out, 'Just over the next hill!' That son of a bitch got lost and we went round and round in circles."

"Hell, that's no dream. We've just been goin' in a great big circle — trekin' up and down those mountains — from here to that German road and back, all for nothing!"

Seward's voice boomed out. "My ass was freezing, and I dreamt I moved over to be closer to my girl. I woke to find I had my arm around old Curry here."

"I was so damn cold that I cuddled up to the 'guy' next to me," Reiss said, "Suddenly I heard some grunting and squealing and found that the warm, tender package next to me was a smelly pig!"

"Hell! Some story! Reiss, you've just had too much of this rakija stuff."

"You son-of-a-buck," yelled Reiss, "Just take my place in the barn tonight and have that pig for your partner."

Stepping outside the bar, Gordon looked at me. "Reiss must be some character."

"He's a tender-hearted guy and a damn good ball turret gunner. Curry was assigned to the ball turret but was scared to death to be cooped up there. Reiss offered to exchange with him, and so Curry moved back to the tail position. Reiss is a big guy to be riding in the ball turret."

"As for Reiss's story, it's true. I slept in the same barn last night. You should've heard the commotion when Reiss found out his sleeping partner was a pig. We got out of there in a hurry."

Hearing voices behind us, we looked back and saw two of our guides talking to a good-looking guy with dark hair, dressed in a spotless, well- pressed German officer's uniform. Clean shaven, he gestured and pointed to us.

61

We looked like a bunch of pack rats. Ripe with fermented sweat and wearing our filthy flying suits, no one could stand to be near us. The young officer smiled and greeted us in English. He told us he was a fighter pilot shot down by our B-17's the day before. We were surprised to hear him speak English and to discover he knew we'd been flying with the 97th bomb group out of Amendola. I wondered if he was the Focke-Wulf pilot who had circled around me the day we bailed out.

We visited with the pilot and discovered he was much like us. He had a family waiting for him in Germany. He was doing his job for the Nazis just as we were doing ours for the U.S. However, regarding our situation with the Partisans there was one big difference. Tito's followers were protecting Allied airmen, but they were fighting the Germans.

The pilot looked at us and smiled. "The war is over as far as we're concerned, fellows." Out of the corner of my eye I saw the Partisans smiling and pointing to the young German.

"The war's over for him, all right," George said.

Later in the day one of our guides was wearing a German pilot's uniform. That young pilot had been such a nice guy.

DAY NINETEEN • WEDNESDAY • APRIL 5

Another day to chew the fat and wonder when the Partisans would move on. Two topics monopolized our conversation — when we would get out of this damn hole — and food.

The longer our stay the more obsessed we became with food. We were always hungry. Waking up in the morning I'd come to the frustrating realization that the fried chicken I'd been eating was only a dream. Later when we ate the watery soup and straw bread, I thought about Mother's freshly baked white bread smothered with strawberry jam, a cold glass of milk, slices of fresh tomatoes sprinkled with sugar. Lying down at night I imagined cutting into a juicy steak or Mother's home-canned beef oozing with rich beef juices, munching a crisp red apple picked from the tree in our backyard, biting into the creamy chocolate of a Hershey bar. We shared imaginary meals with each other, describing our favorites in detail. We never tired of talking about food.

A small piece of sausage with our noon meal made this day in Mrkopolj one to remember. Meat of any kind was a rarity. We made mental note of all foods we were served, but special meals we never forgot.

We were restless and eager to be moving again. This delay only prolonged our discomfort and anxiety. We knew Delnice was nearby, the town where the people had treated us so royally on our way to the coast. Everyone remembered the good food, the dance at the community building and our high expectations of reaching the boat waiting to take us to Italy. While others were complaining about the back-trekking and constant delays, Gordon was talking about Maria, the attractive daughter of our hostess in Delnice. Because of sore feet he couldn't dance with Maria on our first visit, but he bragged he would escort her to a dance this time. We were tired of hearing him talk about his love affair with Maria.

George visited with the Partisans about our leaving Mrkopolj, but the Kommandant said too many other allied airmen were in Delnice and it would not be safe for our group to join them at this time. Tired of hanging out in the town's one bar we strolled past the business houses on Main Street. We bumped into Williamson who was boasting a hair cut and shave.

'Where in the hell did you get a shave?" Brown asked.

Pointing to a building across the street Williamson said, "There's a little man in a shop upstairs who'll give you a shave and hair cut for two dollars."

We looked up and saw a sign in the window above and wondered how Williamson figured out it was a barber shop. News spread quickly and in a short time a line of fellows formed to wait their turn for a shave. This was only the second time we had found a barber since bailing out. With no soap or water for washing, our beards itched from the accumulated dirt and sweat.

A slightly-bald, mustached man grinned as I sat down in his small chair. Picking up a pair of scissors he started cutting my hair, talking a blue streak. This was a big event, for the barber was taking in more dollars in one day than he could normally make in six months. Soap was scarce, and the water was cold, but his razor was sharp and he handled it with bravado. Looking in the cracked mirror I saw a thin face, but at least a clean shaven one. I was grateful for the script money which allowed us this luxury.

Walking outside I heard my name called. The Kommandant had ordered all pilots to appear at Partisan headquarters and help prepare a list of supplies to be radioed to Allied headquarters in Bari. Automatic weapons, ammunition, and medical supplies were essential if the Partisans were to continue fighting the Germans.

Six months before we bailed out, British and American liaison officers parachuted into northern Yugoslavia with radio equipment to establish communication between the Allies and Partisans. In addition to requests for guns and supplies the names and serial numbers of airmen downed in Yugoslavia were relayed to security officers in Bari. Weather information was sent to provide operational officers data in selecting mission targets. Northern Yugoslavia was on the main route to the Ploesti oil fields, so weather conditions in the Balkans were important for planning those missions as well as flights into Germany.

In the guerilla warfare conducted by Tito's men, land frequently exchanged hands between the Partisans and Germans. By radio, Allied officers reported to Bari the kind of materials the Partisans needed and advised them where to drop supplies. Safe landing sites changed from week to week and even from day to day. Allied pilots flew in at night and at a prearranged place dropped ammunition, medicine, and other necessities by parachute. We asked if fields were available where planes could land and take us back to Italy on the return flights. George translated the Kommandant's reply: "No safe landing strips in this mountainous part of Croatia."

DAY TWENTY • THURSDAY • APRIL 6

The next morning, we heard Delnice had been bombed by the Germans. The pilots had also dropped leaflets telling the Croats that German planes would bomb every town on the map. Gordon and I talked about Maria and her family, wondering if they were safe. Was Delnice bombed because the people had given shelter to us? How many innocent people would lose their lives because of us?

Two nights ago, an Allied plane had dropped supplies for the Partisans. We spent most of the morning helping the townspeople haul the ammunition, blankets, boots, and medicines into the headquarters building. At noon the guides rounded up our group and took us to a church located at the far end of main street.

Once inside the church we felt protected and took advantage of the opportunity to remove our sheepskin lined jackets and shirts. Brown and Curry also removed their shoes, glad for a chance to lie down and put their bare feet up on a pew. Two days of no walking had been a godsend. Looking around I noticed that Gordon and Spoon were missing. Spoon no doubt had convinced Gordon to stop at the town bar on their way to the church.

With our shirts off we were better able to hunt down the lice which had been driving us crazy. I'd find one, grab for it, only to find it had escaped my grasp and found another hiding place. We kept a running account of the little buggers, vying with each other to see who could kill the most.

While engaged with chasing lice, we heard the sound of engines. Running outside, we saw an old German single-engine biplane flying above us. Flying at 1000 feet, the plane could be on a reconnaissance mission, sizing up the area for possible build-up of Partisan troops.

The pilot flew south, made a wide sweep toward the east and appeared to be returning to his base. Suddenly he swooped down into the valley, leveled off and came roaring over the town at about 200 feet, strafing and dropping bombs as he headed our direction. The pilot was flying so low we could see him sitting in the open cockpit. We could have hit that plane with a baseball. All hell broke loose as bombs landed only a few yards away, hitting the slate roofs of homes and buildings with a thundering roar. Someone yelled, "My God, we'll be killed!"

We raced to the nearby hills. Carrying their shoes, Brown and Curry ran barefoot in the snow. Completely exposed, we scratched our way higher, distancing ourselves as far as possible from the town. Scared shitless, we threw ourselves on the ground and crouched behind large boulders, as if they could protect us from the bombs.

Looking down on the town below we watched the German plane fly over three more times, strafing and plastering the houses with a volley of bombs. On the final run the pilot dropped incendiary bombs. Houses and buildings were ablaze. As I watched the destruction in the town below, I was overcome with nausea and fear. I'd had the same feeling when we hit an intense tropical storm in the Caribbean on our way to Africa.

Hoping to fly under the weather, I dropped altitude. Conditions were no better. Updrafts and downdrafts jarred the ship and buffeted it about with explosive violence. The rain fell in torrents, flooding the windshield. Flashes of lightning lit up the sky. None of the cross-country flights in the U.S. had prepared me for weather like this. I was responsible for my crew and the plane, and I was scared.

Marion was in radio contact with Beane Field, a small fighter base on the island of St. Lucia. Through my headset I heard the operator in the control tower stating, "You can land, but you'll never take off. The runway is too short for bombers." Nevertheless, I dropped altitude, circled the little island, and we decided to take our chances. St. Lucia is a small mountainous volcanic island. The only place for an airstrip was a narrow stretch between the mountains and the coastline. My vision was hampered by waves of rainwater washing the windshield, but with radio contact from the tower I landed the plane with no trouble.

Personnel at the small air base at St. Lucia had never seen a four-engine bomber on the island, so our takeoff would be the real test. While waiting for the weather to clear we discussed our dilemma with the ground crew and personnel in the tower. Walking the length of the short runway we developed a plan. Reduced weight was essential, so we removed hundreds of boxes of K-rations — our major cargo — and left them for the fellows at Beane Field. Three hours after landing the weather had cleared and we were ready to depart.

The ground crew had pulled our plane so close to the operation buildings that our tail almost touched one of the barracks. As the crew placed blocks in front of the wheels, we applied the brakes and preflighted the engines to takeoff RPM. After several minutes the blocks were removed, I released the brakes and we raced down the runway. Once those engines were revved up, there was no turning back.

When we were at the end of the runway, facing the ocean, I pulled up the landing gear and discovered we were only a few feet above the water. It was our good fortune that the runway had been built on a precipice so once we took off, we had about seventy feet clearance above the water. The elevated location of the runway had been a blessing, for as we lost altitude, we gained airspeed. Skimming over the waves the ship gained momentum and altitude. The prayers from all ten men must have helped lift that plane into the air.

Situations in life over which we have little or no control can be traumatic, whether they be violent storms in the sky or being victims of a strafing on the ground as we'd just been through. None of my crew had crossed the Atlantic or visited countries in Europe or Africa. We had looked forward to getting overseas and doing our part, but these life and death experiences were proving to be more frightful than any of us had ever imagined.

As we started making our way back to town, two fellows approached us, one had a coonskin cap; both were walking barefoot, carrying their flying boots, 'Where the devil have you guys been?" Reiss asked.

"Where else," said Spoon. "Getting clobbered by the Krauts!"

"'Serves you right for going back to that bar."

"In the bar, hell," yelled Spoon. "Gordon and I were hauling the last load of supplies into Partisan headquarters. When we heard all the racket we took for the gully behind the building.

"You'all should've seen Spoon slide into that ravine," laughed Gordon, imitating Spoon's dive. "We both landed in snow up to our knees, filling our doggoned boots with ice water."

Spoon pointed to the town. "The damn explosion was the headquarters building. The ammunition and supplies we all carried went up in smoke."

"The Jerries got the town to burning good."

"Them damn Krauts keep followin' us. They know where we are all the time."

"How much longer can these poor people keep protecting us? They're the ones paying the price."

Silently we made our way back to the village. A thick cloud of smoke hung over the town like a curtain of doom. Where was the mustached barber—the bearded bartender — the Kommandant — the women who had fed us? These people had lost their businesses, their possessions, their homes. Now was the time for us to pitch in and help.

A hut used by the Partisans in the mountains

Yugoslav women salvaging the parachute material

DAY TWENTY-ONE • FRIDAY • APRIL 7

I awakened to orders shouted by our Partisan guides; "Pokret!" — get moving. It was still dark. Looking at my watch I figured we'd slept scarcely four hours. Bone tired from our rugged trip through the mountains at night, we weren't ready for another long trek. The smell of burnt wood was all around us. The smoke had permeated our clothes when we helped the people in Mrkopolj clear up the rubble after the bombing, but now, in Delnice, we couldn't get away from the smell. It was not just our clothes. Delnice had also been bombed and buildings burned.

Gordon wanted to look for Maria, to find out if she had escaped injury. There was no time. After gulping down some bitter coffee the guides hustled us out of the barn and onto a road leading out of town. The men had made a stretcher with two long poles and a blanket for George, who was suffering from Malaria. Feverish and delirious, George seemed too ill to be moved, but because all evadees were to leave the area immediately we couldn't abandon him.

A couple of miles out of town we met seventeen Allied soldiers including two Indians who had fought with the British Colonial Army, two Scotsmen, one soldier from New Zealand, another from Australia, and several from South Africa. We were a mixed lot. Instead of walking they were sitting beside the road, some of them trying to sleep.

An Italian truck came careening around the corner in a cloud of dust. Hearing strains of Italian opera above the motor noise, I recognized the driver as the one who had taken us on the wild ride into Delnice two weeks before. After the fellows in the other group had scrambled into the back end there was no room for us. Noticing our disappointment, the Partisan leader pointed to my watch and put up his forefinger; we would be leaving in one more hour. We looked around for a possible hiding place in case of enemy planes came. The Germans seemed to have spies in every town reporting our whereabouts.

An hour passed. Complaints became more frequent.

"Suppose the crazy Italian forgets all about us."

"It'd be a miracle if that rickety truck could make it back in one piece."

"A greater miracle if the guy doesn't crack up. He pays more attention to his singin' than drivin'."

"So, if he does come, what the hell difference does it make? I'm getting pissed off climbing up and down these mountains, never gettin' anywhere."

"Quit your griping. It's George here who's got something to complain about."

We had no water to quench George's thirst. Burning with fever, he tossed from side to side, and talked about his mother in South Africa — telling her he was safe, and that he'd soon be home. Would he ever make it? Would anyone?

Before the truck came into sight, we could hear the noisy engine. I helped carry George into the back as the others piled on. Remembering the sharp hairpin curves from before and the devil-may-care attitude of our driver, we knew it would be a rough trip. I couldn't decide it if was worse at night in the dark, or by day when we could see how close our driver came to slipping off the road.

When the truck finally stopped, we recognized the burned town as the one where Turk, our "Interpreter" from Gerovo, had left us two weeks before. We looked at each other. If Turk were here, he would never have recognized this ragged bunch of men as those he led down the mountain in the wooden-wheeled kola.

Spring had come to the Kupa valley. Green meadows and flowering trees bordered the river. This wide, well-traveled road was in stark contrast to the narrow, rugged mountain trails packed with snow. I wished I felt better. I had awakened with a gut-ache and now the belly cramps had returned, more severe than ever. The pattern was to walk 55 minutes and rest five. When the pain became acute, I couldn't wait. I ran into the bushes. After several stops, I had fallen behind and was too tired to catch the others, before long, Gordon, Reiss and Brown had joined me. I wasn't the only one suffering from dysentery.

When we met up with our group, we discovered they had joined the British, South African and New Zealand fellows. Most of them had been prisoners of war, released when the Italians surrendered. There were about 40 of us, a large group for villagers to feed. At noon we were given cooked potatoes and raw beets — the main foods left from last year's harvest. Everyone was treated the same. It didn't matter if a person were a Partisan leader, an Allied officer, a POW or an enlisted man. We were all equals, struggling to survive.

The day was sunny and warm, too hot for heavy flight jackets. Dirty as they were, our lined jackets would be prized by any villager, but we couldn't toss them for we needed them at night. The broad Kupa River valley made walking easier, but we were extremely vulnerable to the enemy. Yesterday we had seen at first hand the destruction dealt by only one plane flying over Mrkopolj. On edge after the strafing, we continually searched the sky for planes.

Even though weak from the frequent side trips to the bushes, we took turns carrying George. As Brown and I grabbed the poles, we noticed that George was sweating profusely. He needed medication, but anti-malarial drugs were scarce in the primitive hospitals maintained by the Partisans. Now with his fever broken, George was weak but rational. He asked again and again, "Where are we?" We longed for a map where the guides could point out our position and show us where we were going.

A sudden explosion interrupted the serenity of the peaceful valley. "The doggone Krauts are bombing us again!"

Expecting the worst, everyone dove for cover in an orchard near the road. With George in our care, we were the last to reach the trees. While laying the stretcher on the ground, two of our guides walked towards us, laughing and motioning us to get back on the road. We weren't about to go back and be blown to bits by German snipers.

After talking with the Partisan leader, George explained that one of the young guides had thrown a grenade in the river, just as a joke. All hell broke loose. No language barrier could isolate our guides from the curses yelled by our men. Living as evadees was like flying on a mission that never ended. As targets in German occupied territory, we were continually vulnerable to snipers on the ground and at the mercy of bombs from above. We knew our number could come up anyplace and anytime.

"Where is the f -ing kid? Just let me get my hands on him!"

"The goddamn Jerries will be on our tail for sure now."

Brown and I picked up George and followed our guides to the road. Looking at the river we saw dozens of dead fish floating on the surface. Amused by our reaction to the explosion, our guides set a fast pace and the others soon filed behind. My intermittent cramps continued. I thought I had experienced misery in the mountains, but the combination of dysentery, fear of bombings and keeping up the pace set by our guides had nearly pushed me to the edge.

We were tired of walking, tired of the straw bread and poor food, tired of never knowing where we were or when we would get out. By night nerves were taut and conflicts arose. We were trying to find some warmth and a comfortable spot in the hayloft of a farmer's barn. Spoon's Texas drawl could be heard above the others. "Y'all, get your cotton-pickin' fingers off my blanket."

"By God, I'm keeping it! Where'd you swipe it?"

"Requisitioned it," said Spoon. "Saw it hanging over a fence; I just grabbed it when the damn plane was dropin' its bombs."

"Uh-uh — stole it from the good people in Mkropolj. What kind of thanks is that for the food they gave us?"

Lunging forward with fists upraised Spoon shouted, "Goddammit, give it here."

"Like hell I will."

A fist fight broke out and as leader of our group, Adams walked over and separated the men. Somehow Spoon and Gordon had each found a blanket. Adams said they were theirs to keep. It was cold sleeping in barns but for three weeks we'd kept from freezing with only flight clothes for cover. Now that spring was on its way, we could manage for another few days — or weeks.

DAY TWENTY-TWO • SATURDAY • APRIL 8

Changing of the guard gave us a new set of guides, three young kids. Their uniforms weren't much to look at — frayed German coats and patched trousers that didn't match. Hand grenades hung from their belts and they fingered the highly polished guns on their hips frequently. Mere teenagers, they were old beyond their years, self confident, disciplined, and not afraid to take risks. They wore their Partisan caps with pride.

These young fellows led us on a fast downhill pace. The two Indian boys were jogging out in front, evidently unaffected by the dysentery that continued to bother most of us. With so little to eat we hadn't much inside, but every hour or so we'd have to make a run for the bushes. The squatting relieved the cramping pain in our bellies, temporarily. It was like having the dry heaves, little there, but enough so my rear end was sore as hell.[6]

"How come them Indian guys don't have the runs?" asked Curry.

"Notice how they never touch any food with even a sliver of meat in it?"

"Guess it has something to do with their religion, not eating meat."

"Hell, I don't remember having meat for days and days."

"What about the sausage in Mrkopolj?"

"That was a heck of a small piece to cause this belly ache."

The road led to the broad Kupa River, swollen from spring rains and melting snow. On either side of the river fields were ready for planting. Plum trees were in bloom and little yellow flowers peeked through the grass.

Reaching the river's edge, we slumped to the ground, glad for a chance to rest. We missed George, who as translator had been our unofficial leader. Too sick to walk, he had stayed with the Partisan sympathizers in the last town. Carrying George on a stretcher and keeping up with our guides had been hard on us, but we hated to leave him behind.

The river was running clear and swift, but where was the bridge for crossing? One of the guides pointed to the partly submerged concrete and wooden structure in the middle of the river. We figured out from the guides' sign language that the bridge had been blown up to prevent the Germans from crossing. Fording a wide river with a swift current was out of the question.

---

[6] The cause of dysentery was more than likely from the roots (potatoes, carrots, etc) they ate due to being fertilized with human waste.

Our guides walked over to a saw mill and talked with an old man wearing a ragged sweater and knitted cap. After much waving of arms and talk, the old man disappeared into the mill. In a few minutes he returned with a comrade, carrying a small boat. When the guide motioned for three fellows to get in the boat, we realized this was our transportation. The guys laughed uproariously as Spoon demonstrated crossing the river in a row boat commanded by an oarsman who floundered and turned over in midstream. Always the clown, Spoon in his coonskin cap was good for a laugh when we needed it most.

We allowed the Indians and South Africans to be the first to test the waters. One of the Indians grabbed an oar and with the guide handling the other they started out. The swift current pulled the boat downstream, but they stayed upright. When the boat landed on the far side we cheered.

We sat on the river bank, waiting our turn. Behind us a man was plowing a field with one horse, the way my grandfather plowed his fields in Iowa fifty years ago. The day was warm. We threw off our flight jackets and renewed our fight with the lice. We were never free of lice, teeny tiny buggers running up and down our legs and back, varmits who buried themselves in every crease and crevice. Our guides laughed as we itched, and scratched, and cussed.

It took many trips to transport 40 men across the river in the small boat. With each trip the boat landed farther downstream, so we walked along the bank to keep up.

"I hear planes," said Whiney.

"Whiney's off his rocker again."

Running for cover, Whiney yelled, "Goddammit, those are German planes."

Listening closely, we could hear the faint rumble of engines. Were the planes bombing Delnice again, or another town where the people had given us shelter? We ran into the woods to hide. The Kupa River was a major waterway and anyone on or near the river was vulnerable to attack. Hearing the planes more distinctly we looked through the trees, checking on the position of our boat. On his way back to pick up another load, our guide was a sitting duck.

Two planes came in so low we could see the markings on their bellies. Afraid we'd be clobbered any minute I got a sinking feeling in the pit of my stomach. I heard Reiss repeating his Hail Marys. Seconds passed slowly. As the sound of the engines grew fainter, we looked up and saw the planes fly due east and out of sight. We had lucked out again.

The next crossing was my turn. I knew a lot about cars but nothing about boats, so I was glad when Brown offered to take one of the oars. The heavy wooden vessel was stable and made the trip without mishap. Getting out of the boat was another story for we landed on a sandbank. Our boots sank down six to eight inches in the soft sand and mud. The other guys laughed as we slowly pulled out one foot after the other until we reached firmer ground.

I looked up and saw the Scottish and English fellows nearing the top of a steep cliff. At this bend in the river there was no other way to go but up. Starting up the embankment I slipped backwards two feet while going ahead one, but the going was better when I grabbed some tree roots for support. Waiting at the top were the Indian and South Africans with outstretched hands. No rappelling in basic training had prepared me for conditions like this.

Exhausted from the morning's ordeal, we dragged into the next village. Only our flight clothes were reminders that this ragged band were Air Force men. We thought our gut-ache would leave if we could find something decent to eat, so we went from house to house hoping to buy food with our script money. Four of us walked up to one of the two-story houses and knocked. A lady in a long skirt with a kerchief on her head opened the door. Showing her our money, I said, "Kruh?" She left and returned with a plate of rolls, rolls like my mother makes. White rolls. It couldn't be! We said, "Hvala," over and over trying to convey our sincere appreciation.

After we'd devoured the rolls, the good lady proudly led us to a house across the street to meet her neighbor who had lived in the United States. The neighbor explained that tomorrow was Easter — the most important day in the life of a Catholic. The women in the town had hoarded white flour for months to prepare the traditional Easter kuchen and Croatian cookies made with honey.

From our early encounter with Turk, our interpreter in Gerovo, we had met many men who had worked in America and returned to the home country to retire. Darinka, however, was the first woman we had seen who had lived in the United States. After visiting with us, she went into the kitchen and brought out a plate of cookies and a pitcher of milk. Again, we marveled at the generosity of the people.

With good food and warm hospitality, the long afternoon trek found us in a jovial mood. The men joked, sang umpteen verses of "Lili Marlene", and our own song, "Off we go, into the wild blue yonder..." It wouldn't be long now before we'd be back, for nothing could stop the Army Air Forces!

We walked through many villages, each with its cluster of farmhouses and thatched barns surrounded by bright green meadows. As we came close to a village or town one of the guides would go to scout the area. A couple of times we left the roadway and followed a pasture path. Word was passed along to walk quietly and not to talk. Not all village people were sympathetic to the Partisans. Little news escaped the knowledge of our guides and few enemy secrets were beyond their reach.

Approaching one village we saw a farmer driving his horse and wagon. He smiled and waved. At first glance we assumed he was hauling hay for the Partisans, but as we drew nearer, we found the hay was a camouflage for bags of grain. With spies for both the Ustashi and the Germans in this part of the country, the farmer and countless others risked their lives daily to protect us and support the Partisan cause.

DAY TWENTY-THREE
EASTER SUNDAY • APRIL 9

Easter Sunday. Thoughts of home and family flooded my mind. Easter sunrise service, Easter lilies banking the altar, family gathered around the dinner table for a special meal. War doesn't stop for Christmas or Easter, and only bad weather would have kept us from flying had we been at our base in Amendola.

For us, this Easter was just another day of walking and hoping for a good meal. We never got to see the broad picture of the situation in Yugoslavia. We never found out what was back of the moves, the changes in routes, the failures. Reduced to a narrow screen of sights and sounds we could see only what was affecting us: the Germans attacking at night and preventing us from reaching the Adriatic, their strafing us at Mrkopolj, the Stukas bombing villages or towns the day after we left. We could only hope to get out of here alive, but we had no guarantee and we were scared.

This was rich farmland and we passed through many villages, some no more than a cluster of a few stone cottages. It was planting time but because today was Easter no one was working in the fields. Few cows or sheep were grazing. Armies need food, and either the Germans had seized the animals, or the farmers were forced to give their livestock to the Ustashi or to the Partisans.

Entering a town with a church, shops, and many houses, we were divided into small groups. The people invited us into their homes and shared their Easter dinner with us. For this special meal our guest family had killed their pet rabbit. They insisted we sit at the table while they stood and watched us eat. We felt guilty eating food they had prepared for their Easter dinner. I watched the two children. Tears streamed down the cheeks of the little girl. She would long remember these war years when even her pet rabbit had to be sacrificed for food. I would long remember that Easter dinner, too. The meat tasted like chicken and I was grateful for each bite.

That afternoon we followed a tributary of the Kupa River. Three weeks of walking had taken its toll. My feet were wrapped in rags, my socks had worn out days ago. Brown had used the soft cloth map from his escape kit, but I made do with any scrap I could find.

Peace of this holy day was broken by Whiney running up and down the column of men screaming, "Stukas! Stukas!" Some fellows leaped in the nearest ditch, others took cover in a stand of trees or clump of bushes. Straining our ears, we tried to discover the direction of the planes. Trees, bushes, and ditches offered no protection from bombs. Yesterday the planes passed over us. Would we be so lucky again?

When our guides approached us and gave the command to start walking we realized it was a false alarm! Whiney was compelled to draw attention to himself one way or another. Yesterday his warning was real, but today's deception was too much. He got attention all right. A half dozen fellows ganged up on him and would have killed him if the Partisan guides had not pulled them away.

The sun had set, and we were still walking. It was eight o'clock before we reached the city of Metlika where we were divided into groups of two or four for the evening meal. Our hosts served us ham, wine, and kuchen, traditional Easter bread made with white flour. Two meals in one day!

DAY TWENTY-FOUR • MONDAY • APRIL 10

I awoke with hay in my hair and nostrils. Some of the guys were fighting again. Barns in this part of the country were large and provided plenty of hay. Even though the temperature dropped at night, hay plus the many bodies crowded together helped to keep us warm.

I reached for my boots. We usually slept with them on, ready for a quick escape in case the Germans were near, but after two days of steady walking my feet were killing me. Blisters had broken open again and were bleeding. I dreaded putting boots back on without socks. I was tying my shoes when someone yelled, "Pokret," which meant, get off your butts and get moving.

Walking into town we talked about our situation and wondered if this could be our final destination. Metlika was a large town with many shops and impressive two-story stucco homes with red-tiled roofs. The brick streets were clean and there was no evidence of bombings or burned homes. I felt as if I were in one of our Midwestern towns in the States, safe from snipers and sneak bomb attacks.

The surrounding rich farmland was reflected in the obvious prosperity of the town's inhabitants. We met several people who had lived in the United States and could speak English. They didn't agree with the Communist's policy of "share and share alike." In this agricultural area the Communists had taken much of the farmers' grain and livestock to feed Tito's army. The people weren't happy about giving up their crops, but they didn't want to collaborate with the Germans.

Spoiled by yesterday's good meals, we ran down the streets trying to be the first ones in the shops. When we found bread and food for sale, we went crazy, handing out our script money like there was no tomorrow. Four of us got a large muslin sack and bought as much food as we could find. In the shop a lady boiled fifty eggs for us. We dumped them in the sack with a half dozen loaves of bread. Walking through town we saw a city park with benches. Stopping to rest we put down our sack and tore open a loaf crusty dark bread, each grabbing our share. Fresh bread, onions, and boiled eggs. We could have eaten everything on the spot, but our better judgment told us we'd better save something for tomorrow.

One of the young guides directed us to the Partisan headquarters' building. Once again, I gave the Kommandant the names, home addresses and serial numbers of my crew. This routine had become a familiar one in the larger towns, and I hoped by now our parents had been notified that we were alive. I was worried about my family. If mother had received no word in three weeks, she would be sure I had been killed.

Finishing my work, I noticed that many of the fellows had left the room and walked outside. I saw our guys talking to a tall, clean-shaven officer in a spotless British uniform. A British captain in Yugoslavia! We couldn't believe our good fortune to find someone in authority who could speak English. For weeks we had been starved for food, but even more starved for news about our getting out.

We hounded him with questions. Introducing himself as Captain Eden, he told us he had parachuted into Slovenia a few weeks ago. He explained that he was an emissary from the British to Tito and was to assist in helping escaped POWs and downed Allied airmen. The guys were slapping each other on the back and shouting, "Yea! We'll be out in a day. Back to the good, old USA!"

Walking over to the captain, Gordon took off his leather flying boots and showed him the welts and blisters on his feet. "How about some real shoes? Got any of those?" When Eden saw the men wearing flight boots, he sent one of the Partisans into the headquarters building. The aid returned with an armload of shoes, and the guys rushed to get a pair.

"How about socks?" I asked.

"No socks, only shoes and wool clothing," replied Eden. I made a mental note that next time a Partisan Kommandant asked me to write our names I would request a supply of socks. Looking over the shoes Gordon said. "These look like GI boots. Where'd you get 'em?" Eden explained they were British boots and had been dropped by parachute a few nights before along with medical supplies and ammunition. So, our planes were getting through with provisions for the Partisans. Brown stepped up. "When's the next plane out, sir?"

Brown had asked the sixty-four-dollar question. All talking ceased. Everyone anxiously awaited Captain Eden's reply. "Sorry, but the blimey planes don't land here. They only drop supplies by parachute."

In groups of two or three, the fellows walked away, trying to hide their disappointment. Those who found shoes were putting them on. After lacing up his shoes, Spoon started jigging on the cobbled street, grinning and calling out, "Can't you guys dance?"

DAY TWENTY-FIVE • TUESDAY • APRIL 11

As we returned to our sleeping quarters in the barn outside of town we were accompanied by Partisan soldiers, both men and women. Finding places on the barn floor, four Partisan boys and three Partisan girls slept side by side in a row. Nobody thought anything about it. Women as well as men were considered soldiers on an equal basis and governed by the same strict rules. No sex.

We looked up Captain Eden in the morning, hoping he'd give us some specific information about our getting out. When asked, he was evasive. Some of my crew were grumbling, "He doesn't know as much about the Partisans as we do."

"And we don't know any more about getting out than we did before we met this English guy. What goes?"

"He can't tell us nothing because it's the Partisans who are calling the shots."

Trying to excuse Captain Eden I said, "Maybe he's with British Intelligence and can't reveal plans."

Tired of pumping Eden with questions and getting no straight answers, we checked in at Partisan headquarters to see if those guys would tell us anything. Opening the door, the first person I saw was George. My crew joined in a rousing cheer. Lifting his right hand with a V for victory sign George said, "You won't be leaving me behind again. Bet you had a hard time getting along without me."

Brown broke in, "Sure have. Can you tell us, is this English officer going to get us out of here?"

"I don't think there's much Eden can do as far as getting us out. Tito and his officers are calling the shots and they're Communists. They don't trust the British because they've been slow to support the Partisans.

"But if Tito's troops are to continue fighting the Germans, they need medical supplies, clothing and food. This is where Eden comes into the picture. With his wireless he can radio the British and make arrangements for supply drops. He can get information on the Partisan movements, what guns and ammunition they need and how successful they are in fighting the Germans. He can also alert the Allies concerning possible bombing targets, the major railroads and routes being used by the Germans to transport troops and supplies.

"As for us getting out of this country, the Partisans are still our lifeline. They're the only ones who know where the enemy is and can protect us from being captured. They aren't telling any secrets. Their success depends upon tight security."

Brown looked up, "So this means more walking, I suppose."

"You're right," said George. "No safe landing sites for planes in this part of the country."

We were taken to a schoolhouse where several women dished polenta out of large kettles into soup dishes. Another group of airmen had joined us. With more fellows the food had to stretch further so we couldn't ask for seconds, but the chance to visit with fellow airmen helped to make up for the shortage of food. We were always eager to see new guys, hear their stories and find out what they knew about our chances of getting out.

About two in the afternoon we received marching orders. We were a large group now, almost eighty plus the 200 Partisan soldiers who were accompanying us. We figured there must be lots of Germans near since the Partisans had assigned us so many soldiers.

We walked until six o'clock, following cow paths and narrow roads. I caught up with Gordon, "How are the new shoes?"

"A little stiff," said Gordon, "but better than those floppy flight boots."

As we entered a small village, the people pointed at us and shouted angrily. George said they were blaming us for taking their food, for losing their men and women to the Partisan army. They claimed the Ustashi would burn their houses and kill them if they gave us shelter.

We walked to the outskirts of town and spent the night in a barn, glad for the milder weather and the eggs, onions and bread in our sack.

DAY TWENTY-SIX • WEDNESDAY • APRIL 12

I awoke to arguing and fighting. Williamson was shouting and ranting about the thieves in our midst. Almost everyone had bought bread in Metlika and carried some on the trek east. For two days Williamson had been hoarding his bread inside the ripped lining of his coat. By evening he had a half- loaf remaining, so for safe-keeping he had slipped it inside his boots which he used for a pillow. When he awakened the bread was gone. With fist clenched he demanded someone return the bread, but his ravings produced nothing but retaliation from the other guys.

We were all starving. We greedily ate anything that looked like food. I couldn't get enough of the straw bread and watery soup I'd found so disgusting those first few days. While swallowing the last bite of a meager meal we were already thinking about the next one. In the four weeks we'd been with the Partisans we'd never had a square meal. We began to resemble the thin, haggard people whom we saw in the villages. We were so crazed for food any of us could have stolen another man's bread without any feeling of remorse.

"Hey, George. You told us about the Partisans who were shot for stealing food. Tell the guys. Stealing Williamson's bread could be a serious offense."

"One of the guides," said George, "told me about two Partisan soldiers who entered a house and forced a woman to give them food. She went to the Partisan headquarters and complained. The two soldiers were summoned before the battalion. They admitted what they had done and were condemned to death.

"Before being shot one of the men said, 'Comrades, I consider the punishment to be just. I have committed a grave crime. Our brigade has gone from one end of Yugoslavia to the other, liberating one city after the other from the invader. We are the Army of Liberation and I have soiled its name. Shoot me because the punishment must be imposed."

Spoon said, "To be shot for taking a little food? I'd mutiny."

George continued. "The Partisans' main support comes from the population. Where would you fellows be if the Partisans hadn't found villagers who would take you in, give you shelter and food? The people in the towns who give aid to the Partisan cause are as much a part of Tito's Army as those men and women who are fighting. Any conflict with the people could mean the end of the struggle against the invaders. There is a Chinese proverb that says: 'Partisans among the people are like fish in a river. The river can live by itself — but not the fish."

The day was bright and sunny. Trees were framed by the blue hills and snow-covered mountains. No reason to spoil the day over someone's stolen food.

We walked over to a meadow covered with short, bright green grass, the kind that announces the coming of spring. We lay down to rest and looked up at the puffs of clouds skimming across the sky. Others joined us, soaking in the peace and quiet. The ground was still cold, but the sun warmed us. For the moment the war seemed a long way off.

Our dreams were interrupted by the sound of thunder in the distance and excited shouts from behind us, "Avioni! Avioni!" The Partisans were waving their arms and pointing. High above, thin trails of white smoke combed the sky. At the head of the vapor trails we could make out our bombers gilded by the sun. One formation followed another. Weaving in and out were fighter escorts, shining and twisting like silver fish around the Fortresses and Liberators. With broad smiles the Partisans repeatedly called out, "Nasi, Nasi!" Already they were claiming Allied aircraft as theirs. We wondered about the possible target — Ploesti oil fields? Sofia? Someplace in Yugoslavia?[7]

The vapor trails from hundreds of bombers made a spectacular sight. We watched with awe and wonderment as group after group made their way across the sky to the northeast. Seeing our planes gave us a lonely feeling. The guys up there would be back at the base, eating in the mess hall and sleeping on our cots in a warm tent. We yearned to be part of the war up there at 20,000 feet, above the fighting and misery on the ground.

Our guides motioned it was time to move. We fell in line behind about a hundred soldiers who had started walking down a cow path. Another hundred or so followed. The troops, dressed in old clothes or captured Italian or German uniforms, were armed with grenades at their belts. Many carried rifles. We were still in the hills, but the walking was easier. Before long the soldiers broke out in song, singing as though all the world was happy and the war was already won. The miracle of Yugoslavia was the indomitable spirit of their people.

---

[7] On April 12, B-17s with the Fifteenth Air force bombed marshalling yards and an air drome in Zagreb

After walking several hours, we approached a cluster of stone cottages. One of the Partisan women went ahead to scout the area and determine the sympathies of the villagers. In a short time, she returned with two English officers dressed in well-pressed uniforms and polished shoes. Their neat appearance was in stark contrast to our disheveled hair, unwashed beards, and dirty flight suits.

The short, older, mustached officer wore a black patch over one eye. He introduced himself as Major Jones and his younger companion as Lt. Col. Moore. Both men were British liaison officers with the Partisans. We learned that Major Jones had parachuted into Slovenia the previous May and was the first officer with the British Mission to be affiliated with Tito's Partisans. A member of the Black Watch of Canada, he had lost an eye fighting in World War I. Eager for more action he volunteered to parachute into the Balkans and live with the Partisans. Jones spoke German fluently and had picked up enough Croatian words, so he could converse with the people. The Partisans trusted Major Jones.

Major Jones saluted and addressed the Partisan leader, "Smrt Fasizmi!" The leader replied in kind. We fired questions at the Colonel and Major. "What's up?"

"When can you get us out?"

Major Jones stretched out his hand, "Colonel Moore and I'll be accompanying you for the next few days. We've been over this route before, but it's the Partisans who will see us through. Follow their orders implicitly."

"How come all these guys are putting their necks on the line for us?"

Major Jones continued. "The Partisans are protecting you because we have a common enemy. The people of Yugoslavia have been oppressed all their lives. They have a burning desire for a better life and see Tito as the embodiment of their hopes and dreams. They've mobilized the youth, the women — even the aged. They've created a fighting force and a support system among the villagers beyond anything we have ever seen. The common people here have never had a chance. Now the time has come when they have hopes of gaining independence and freedom."

"But I thought these guys were Communists."

"Tito and the men who plan the strategy and give the orders are Communists. But the Partisan movement is also a peasant rebellion. Tito represents the common man. To follow him is a way of escape for a people who have been ruled by despots for centuries. The occupation of the country by the Germans has merely intensified existing troubles.

"You are lucky to be in the hands of the Partisans. They are ruled by rigid discipline and follow orders without question. They will kill anyone not sympathetic with the Partisan cause, but they'll risk death to protect you."

With their reassurances, Colonel Moore and Major Jones had given us the shot in the arm we needed. They gave us hope that we would make it through. We fell back in line and by evening reached a small village.

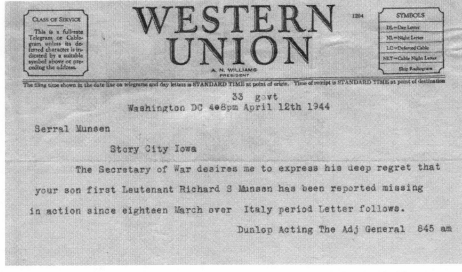

Telegram sent to Dick's parents on April 12th, 1944 - 26 days after bailing out.

DAY TWENTY-SEVEN • THURSDAY • APRIL 13

We always felt better when the order, Pokret, came early in the morning. Nothing hurt our morale more than lying around, doing nothing. The day was bright and the snow on the mountains sparkled in the sun. When we flew over this country on missions, Reiss had a panoramic view from the ball turret and often bragged that he was going to see these mountains some day. "It looked so beautiful from up there I vowed when the war was over, I'd come back and visit this country."

Sully piped up. "So, you're the one responsible for our being down here. I've seen enough goddamn mountains for a lifetime. All we've done is walk up one and down another."

With only a little polenta for breakfast I was wondering when we would eat. I dreamed of my first meal in the states — fried chicken so tender it falls off the bone, mashed potatoes swimming in gravy and a cold glass of milk. Would that day ever come?

Behind me Reiss was carrying on a heated conversation with Curry. Reiss was curious. "Whacha got in the can?"

"Somethin' Lieutenant Williamson told me to carry." said Curry.

"You mean Williamson ordered you to carry it? That means he gave it to you."

"Oh, no," said Curry. "He wants to keep it — just wanted me to carry it for a while."

"Hell, here's what we're going to do. Give me that can. You've got a pocket knife, haven't you?"

"You ain't goin' to open it?"

"The hell I ain't!"

"Reiss, he'll kill me!"

Reiss grabbed the can from Curry. "No. I took it from you. Remember? I'll take care of that son of a buck."

Holding the can up to his nose, Reiss grinned. "It's mackerel all right, I can smell it. I can see it, too, — rich, juicy tender pieces oozing with oil, just waiting to be eaten."

When we stopped for our five-minute rest, I walked over to Reiss and asked, "What's the problem with you and Curry?"

Reiss related the situation. "We're all starving and Williamson orders Curry to carry this can of mackerel for him. He's tired of lugging it around. What's Williamson hoarding it for? A souvenir? Saving it for himself? Hell. I took a pocket knife, opened the can and we ate the whole thing. Never had anything that tasted so good."

I could see the tell-tale signs of fish oil dripping down Reiss's chin. "Reiss, you'll have to deal with Williamson. If you need support, count me out. If anyone had seen you fellows eating that mackerel they would've half killed you to get their share."

"By Golly, Munsen, a guy'll do anything to survive."

Our faces were thin and drawn. Our clothes hung on us. Starvation does crazy things to people. We couldn't think of anything but food. I could understand why Reiss and Curry ate the mackerel, but I didn't want to be around when Williamson found out.

We had passed several villages. For assistance in feeding our large group the Partisans needed to know the loyalties of each village. About eleven o'clock we received the command to stop. Within the hour the women served us a soup made from potatoes, cabbages and onions. Although it was mostly water it helped to fill an empty stomach.

I walked over to the group of men gathered around Major Jones and Colonel Moore. We looked across the road where the soldiers were eating their meal. It was the same food we were served. Because of their common goal of freedom, all kinds of people, from professionals to farmers, had joined the Partisan struggle, but they were all treated the same. This was democracy in action.

Gordon joined us. "What's up? Why all the soldiers? There must be two hundred of 'em."

Major Jones answered. "The Germans control both Zagreb and Karlovac, their air fields and railroads. The Karlovac-Zagreb road is a major route for shipping German troops and supplies. Tonight, we cross both the road and railroad. Right now, we're in a tight squeeze, about half-way between the two towns. These soldiers are here in case the Germans cause trouble. We're a large group to sneak through German lines. Spies are everywhere."

Brown turned to Colonel Moore. "Can you get us out, that is after we've crossed the German road?"

"The Partisans know the country and the enemy's positions. Trust them. We can't go with you all the way. Major Jones and I are here to help facilitate the flow of supplies and ammunition from Italy into the hands of the Partisans so they can fight this war. As British liaison officers we travel with Tito's approval."

Major Jones interrupted. "There are a couple of places where planes can land and take you fellows out, but in the guerilla war they're fighting, the front changes week to week, sometimes day to day. This is Tito's show. His men take full responsibility for guiding you through their country."

Even though the Partisans were still in command, we were excited to have Allied officers with us. We'd had George, who could translate, but to have two British officers, who could speak English and were working to get us out, restored our hope. George had been visiting with the Commander of the Partisan brigade and stopped by to tell us this was a good time to sleep. "We won't be moving until after dark and it'll be a long walk."

I lay down, but sleep wouldn't come. Every combination of possible disaster went through my mind. How could the Partisans help us against the Germans? They had no planes and little artillery. This was our first attempt to cross a major German road since the infamous night the Germans were warned by the barking dog. After weeks of walking, hiding, and walking some more we had finally reached the incredible obstacle that had eluded us for so long. German spies were everywhere, maybe even in this small village. It was better to get moving and think of something else. I found Brown and we walked around, checking out the little village.

There were only a few houses and they were small, some with thatched roofs, quite different from the two story, red-tiled homes in Metlika. Walking further we saw two women carefully sweeping the ground on one side of their cottage. They placed logs of wood on the cleaned area and started a fire. Attracted by the bonfire, we stayed to watch.

When the wood was well burned, the coals were swept to the side, leaving the ground hot but clean. One of the women brought out an immense cast-iron bowl. Looking closer we saw it was filled with bread dough, kneaded and shaped into a large round loaf. She placed the dough on the ground, blackened from the hot coals, and covered it with the heavy bowl. Taking a small shovel in hand, the woman heaped the hot coals on top of the cover. So this was the way they baked their coarse, brown bread. We had to admit it had its advantages. We hadn't brushed our teeth since we were shot down but they were white and clean.

We met George who was talking to the Commander, a man in his thirties, tall, with thick, unruly black hair. Although in charge of the brigade he wore no medals and no badges. In fact, we never saw Partisans wear insignia to identify their rank. The soldiers were cleaning their guns. The Partisans' equipment left much to be desired, but the rifles, many confiscated from the Germans and Italians, were kept meticulously clean. Machine guns, too, were being tuned for battle. Sentries had taken their posts and returned at intervals to report German activity.

The Commander told George that yesterday's Allied bomber mission had succeeded in stopping the trains going to Karlovac, at least temporarily. Already the Germans were repairing the tracks, but the Commander was optimistic about our crossing the road safely.

After dark we heard the command to march. We numbered about eighty evadees, a large group for a risky mission. About a hundred soldiers went ahead of us and another hundred behind, many carrying rifles and everyone wearing belts heavy with clusters of hand grenades and cartridge pouches. There were women as well as men, but it was the latter who took turns pulling the machine guns on their heavy tripods.

Only with intimate knowledge of the terrain was it possible to move in the dark from one place to another without colliding with the enemy. The Partisans knew every small piece of forest, every bluff, each turn in the path. Each mile had its own degree of danger and demanded appropriate consideration. We lived from one hour to the next, our lives narrowed down to the essential problem of survival.

After a couple of hours, we saw a soldier holding a guy by the neck. Another Partisan had his gun aimed at him. No doubt a spy, George said. He was a Ustashi, one of the rabid Croats who were fanatical anti-communists and often fought side by side with the Germans. After interrogation he would be dead. We were told the Partisans killed all their enemies: Germans, Chetniks, Ustashi. Only Allied airmen and POWs received protection.

Usually we rested five minutes out of every hour, but tonight we couldn't afford that luxury. In single file, we moved quietly. Not a sound was heard along the line of march. Security depended upon concealment and silence.

We knew we were approaching the railroad when we saw a blue spotlight. The enemy heavily patrolled the road and the railroad, day and night. We waited, lying down in the wet grass a hundred yards from the road, hardly breathing. Scouts were carefully positioned but we could see the German patrol checking the area in their armored jeep.

When the jeep rolled out of sight the command to move was whispered from one man to another. Group by group, we dashed across the road, ran a few hundred feet, climbed an embankment, crossed the railroad and headed for the fringe of beech trees where we fell prostrate on the ground.

We had made it. And not a gun had been fired.

WAR DEPARTMENT

THE ADJUTANT GENERAL'S OFFICE

WASHINGTON

IN REPLY
REFER TO
AG 201 Munsen, Richard S.
PC-N NATOCO

13 April 1944.

Mr. Serral Munsen,

Story City, Iowa.

Dear Mr. Munsen:

This letter is to confirm my recent telegram in which you were regretfully informed that your son, First Lieutenant Richard S. Munsen, 0-803,850, Air Corps, has been reported missing in action since 18 March 1944 over Italy.

I know that added distress is caused by failure to receive more information or details. Therefore, I wish to assure you that at any time additional information is received it will be transmitted to you without delay, and, if in the meantime no additional information is received, I will again communicate with you at the expiration of three months. Also, it is the policy of the Commanding General of the Army Air Forces upon receipt of the "Missing Air Crew Report" to convey to you any details that might be contained in that report.

The term "missing in action" is used only to indicate that the whereabouts or status of an individual is not immediately known. It is not intended to convey the impression that the case is closed. I wish to emphasize that every effort is exerted continuously to clear up the status of our personnel. Under war conditions this is a difficult task as you must readily realize. Experience has shown that many persons reported missing in action are subsequently reported as prisoners of war, but as this information is furnished by countries with which we are at war, the War Department is helpless to expedite such reports. However, in order to relieve financial worry, Congress has enacted legislation which continues in force the pay, allowances and allotments to dependents of personnel being carried in a missing status.

Permit me to extend to you my heartfelt sympathy during this period of uncertainty.

Sincerely yours,

ROBERT H. DUNLOP
Brigadier General,
Acting The Adjutant GENERAL

Letter sent from the War Department to Dick's father, Serral Munsen.

DAY TWENTY-EIGHT • FRIDAY • APRIL 14

Faint streaks of light appeared in the east, outlining the range of mountains. We longed for the morning and the command to halt. Because of danger, we had not been allowed the usual five-minute rest stops. In the dim light I could make out a few small cottages and thatched barns in the distance. Surely now we could eat and rest.

I noticed a Partisan talking excitedly to Major Jones and waving his arms. Warning us to be quiet, the word, "Tishina" was whispered down the line. News had spread that we had crossed the Zagreb/Karlovac road. With the Germans and Ustashi heavily patrolling the area we were forced to stay in the hills. As most of the Partisan soldiers had returned to their regular units, it was back to the rugged mountain trails.

After following a rocky path along the steep banks of a river we crossed the stream, sloshing through the shallowest part. Once on the other side we climbed another hill and finally heard the call to rest. I flopped on the ground, so tired I couldn't drag myself another step. If a German tank appeared over the hill they could come and get me.

But when the five-minute rest period was up, and the order came to march, I got up and shuffled along. Nothing would be worse than being left behind. We by-passed another village and started crossing a broad green meadow bordered by beech trees. The pace increased, and I hustled to keep up.

After reaching the trees, we heard the sound of a powerful engine. Our gut reaction was to run, but the guides motioned for us to hit the dirt. Flat on the ground, we clung to the earth while a plane roared over the tree tops, swooped down over the meadow and zoomed up again. The pilot flew back and forth, casing the area, trying to flush us out like a flock of migrating birds.

We were fearful the pilot had seen our tracks in the meadow grass, fresh with morning dew. He evidently saw no signs and didn't waste ammunition on an empty field. As the noise of the plane disappeared in the distance not a sound could be heard but the heavy breathing of those around me.

As I lay on the ground, clutching the grass with my hands, I thought of the scary situations we'd experienced. Even before we bailed out and found ourselves in this country infested with Germans, we had encountered trouble.

Our flight across the Atlantic, from Brazil to Africa, was beset with problems. First, we hit a tropical storm, so high and so wide we couldn't fly above or around it. Our heavy bomber shuddered as it was buffeted violently upward, nose high.

93

The wheel had almost been wrenched from my grasp as I struggled to get the nose down and the wings level. Forced to drop altitude, we were soon skimming above the water. Lightning lit up the rain-flooded windshield.

Flying through a thunderstorm is a frightful experience. The danger of being struck by a bolt of lightning is always imminent. Almost expecting the bad news, I heard Curry shouting over the intercom, "The ship's on fire!" Sheets of blue flame had formed along the edge of the wings and spread rearward. Another flame played back and forth on the radio antennae and over the nose with a weird and terrifying effect. The propellers looked like pinwheels on a fireworks display. Rain continued to beat against our ship. We had another 1000 miles of ocean to cross before reaching Africa.

Miraculously, the engines didn't miss a beat and the plane was not affected by the streams of electrical flames that built up along the edges of the wing, broke loose, and flew to the rear. In about an hour, the most severe storm had passed. It wasn't until later that we learned we had experienced Saint Elmo's fire, a curious manifestation of static electricity.

Terrifying as the storm had been, we were now faced with another problem. The storm had thrown us off course. It was essential we hit the bulge of Africa with some exactness, for to the north were Messerschmitts and to the south the land receded too far west to reach it with our diminished fuel supply. To prevent the Germans from detecting us, we were forced to maintain radio silence. Shapiro, our navigator, calculated and recalculated our position, reporting every few minutes. Spoon had transferred all fuel from our auxiliaries to the main tanks. When the fuel ceased to be visible in the glass sight tubes, we knew we had only fifty gallons remaining in each of the four main tanks, enough for forty to fifty minutes of air time.

It had been a tense situation. Slowly the minutes had ticked by. Perspiration ran down my face and neck with my shirt glued to my back. It was Shapiro in the astrodome who first announced he saw a haze along the horizon. Peering ahead, Williamson finally cried out, "That's land! It's land!"

By that time Marion was in radio contact with the tower at Dakar and we knew we were within fifty miles of the air field. Even that scary ordeal over the Atlantic paled in comparison to being hunted down by the Germans in Yugoslavia.

The guide called out, telling us to get moving. The German Heinkel had left, but before long we heard bombing in the distance. It was the same old pattern. The Germans were always on our tail, bombing villagers who had protected us. How many towns would the Germans destroy while looking for us? How many innocent people would suffer because of us?

We got up and walked two more hours, passing several bomb craters and shattered carcasses of ponies, proof of what could have happened had we been caught in the open. Switchbacks led to a small village. People were curious but smiled warmly. Several of the children and women wore dresses of green, yellow and white, the same shades as our parachutes. Relieved to hear they would give us shelter we lay down and slept.

We awoke to the smell of food. Women were handing out straw bread and serving soup cooked in large iron pots on an open fire. I hurried to get in line, for with over eighty of us descending on this little village I wondered if there would be enough food to go around.

Walking to the edge of the village Brown and I met Gordon and Spoon. They pointed to part of our gang crowded around a clump of trees. Gordon called out. "There's water coming out of that pump. Better get in line."

We hurried over. Finally, able to elbow my way through, it felt good to splash the water on my face and get some of the grime off my beard. Even better was pouring some of the clear, cold water on my blistered feet.

"I wish somebody'd rig up a shower," said Brown.

"Hell," replied Spoon, "if you go long enough without a bath even the fleas will let you alone."

We gathered in the main street of the town, shooting the breeze and wondering when we'd start walking again. About dusk a dilapidated truck rattled into town. George had mentioned we might have transportation, but this vehicle looked like it had already made its last trip. The villagers chattered excitedly. This was a special occasion for them. We looked at the wooden platform with a stake rack and wondered how many of us would be left behind.

An old lady grasping a shawl tightly under her chin came up and talked to George. He told us her story. Three Ustashi had broken down the door of her house, slit her husband's throat and after raping her daughter, shot her. Hiding in the loft, the horrified woman witnessed the atrocities. When the murderers left, she ran to a neighbor's home for help. Grief-stricken, she was pleading for a ride so she could look for her son, a Partisan soldier.

As Major Jones climbed in front with the driver, our guide motioned for us to get into the truck. About half of us were herded in back — sweaty, dirty, lice-ridden men — squeezed together like so many cords of lumber. The Partisans decided there was room for the old lady, who crawled up to join us. We said good bye to Colonel Moore and the other guys who were waiting for another vehicle. As usual we didn't know where we were or where we were going, but riding was sure better than walking.

The driver cranked the engine energetically and the truck leaped forward. It was a wild ride on the mountain roads. Laboring up the steep hills, the truck went down the crooked roads at break neck speed, the back end swerving perilously. When we reached a curve, everyone leaned the opposite way to keep the sides from falling off. After bouncing over an especially rough road, the engine coughed — and died. Everyone piled out, glad for some breathing space. The bad news was the truck was out of gas. Stranded in the mountains we assumed we would start walking, but after a long wait another truck appeared on the scene.

"Give the Partisans credit," said Major Jones. "Tito's men follow orders implicitly and get things done. They never quit."

The driver had the engine running before everyone had climbed in the back end. He dared not delay for when the sun came up there was danger of being strafed. Ours was a race between time and daylight.

DAY TWENTY-NINE • SATURDAY • APRIL 15

We woke about noon and went looking for food. Forty airmen suddenly descending on the town caused quite a stir. The food vendors were doing a brisk business. Brown and I found an old lady who had set up a little stand on the street and was selling roast pork. Real meat! Curry came by with a loaf of bread and the food was devoured in minutes. The townspeople were thankful for our script money, and we were grateful for meat.

We walked across the street to chat with Major Jones. Saluting, we asked him where we were.

"This is Slunj. About 60 kilometers south of Karlovac."

"Sixty! Seems like two hundred since we crossed the railroad."

"We've traveled a fair piece since then all right — forced into the hills when the Stuka flew over."

"What's the scoop? Any more German roads to cross?"

"Only one, and then you'll be flown to Italy."

We were surprised to see George walk over with two young soldiers in German uniform. They were not prisoners of war, he explained, but Croats who had been forced to join the German army. One had been trained as a mechanic, the other as a pilot. They had run away from their division in Austria and found their way back to Croatia via Tito's underground, much as we were doing. They showed Major Jones their ration cards to prove their good standing with Tito's Army of Liberation. With so many spies, and factions, careful interrogation was necessary for the Communists to determine who was loyal and who would turn around and knife you in the back.

Roaming around the town we ran into Sully and Reiss. Sully was smoking a cigarette!

"By God, Sully, where'd you steal the cigarettes?"

"Steal them! I bought 'em in the store over yonder."

"What's the brand, Yugoslav Special?"

"Grape leaf special," chimed in Reiss. "Sully'd take anything he could smoke."

Pulling out a small drawstring bag from his pocket, Sully showed us his substitute tobacco, finely ground up grape leaves.

"How do they taste?"

Sully grinned. "Ah, they're great!"

Sully would never admit how awful they tasted, but seeing the tears roll down his cheeks when he took a drag told the real story.

At dusk the truck pulled up and we climbed in. We wondered why the Partisans were transporting us by truck. Maybe a large group on foot was more likely to be noticed by the enemy. After an hour the truck stopped. We hoped the guides had checked the gas tank this time. Climbing out the back, we saw a cable stretched across the road about five feet from the ground. If a jeep or motorcycle came tearing down the road, the driver could be injured, even decapitated. This inexpensive method of defense was another example of Partisan ingenuity. Almost an hour passed before the cable was removed and replaced so it was again in position to do its job.

Toward midnight the truck stopped again. It was time for Major Jones to leave us. He had good news. "In three more days you'll be near a field where C-47s can land. In four days, you should be in Italy. Good-bye and good luck."

Our ordeal would soon be over. Within the hour the truck careened into a town or at least a place that had been a town. In the darkness we could barely see the outlines of walls and a few chimneys.

Exhausted we fell on the floor of a burned house and went to sleep.

DAY THIRTY • SUNDAY • APRIL 16

When we awoke we discovered the awful destruction. Four scorched stone walls, with an old canvas slung over the top, had been our shelter. Around us blackened chimneys stood ghost-like, the only remains of former houses. Broken crosses gave evidence of a bombed-out structure that had been a church. The acrid smell of burning wood and flesh hung over the village. The destruction by the enemy sneered at us from every turn.

Children peeked from behind a wall that had once been a house. Several women and an old man were dragging a few charred boards, salvaging any useful materials. Their gaunt faces showed hardship and starvation. These village people were suffering the privations of war just as the men and women at the front. Theirs was a revolution at the grass roots against tyranny. Willing to make the ultimate sacrifice, they expected to gain independence from authoritarian rulers and be at peace in their villages. We, too, wanted this miserable war to be over, to return to our loved ones.

Farther down the street we saw some of our group gathered around the charred remains of a building. We were dumbfounded to see human faces at near ground level framed by bars. Crammed into a dirty hole in the ground were men — not Germans, but Yugoslavs.

Gordon asked, "Who are these men, caged like animals?"

"Could be Chetniks," said Brown.

While pointing at the men, one of the guides said, "White Guards." Curious, I went to find George, hoping he could explain.

"The guide says these men who burned the town are White Guards," I said.

"He's right," George explained. "Some people call them White Guards, but they're really the Ustashi. They burned this town, and many others. The Ustashi are more hated by Tito's men than the Chetniks. They're Croats, pro-German radicals. Their name, White Guards, implies their belief in ethnic superiority, a take-off of Hitler's master race ideology.

"The common procedure of the Ustashi is to enter a town suspected of being sympathetic to Tito's Partisans, torture and kill the inhabitants, and burn the village. Arriving late on the scene of this atrocity, a Partisan brigade captured about thirty Ustashi involved in the killings. Tito's men will show no mercy. After interrogation the men will be killed."

It wasn't only the Chetniks who opposed the Partisans but the Ustashi as well — all Yugoslavs, brother killing brothers.

"What if my radio operator was picked up by the Ustashi. Would he be killed?" I asked.

"He'd probably be turned over to the Germans in which case he'd be in a German POW camp," George replied. "We're lucky to be under command of the Partisans, for they know the safety zones in this country, areas not controlled by the Ustashi or Chetniks. More important the Partisans are in contact with the Allied officers like Major Jones and Colonel Moore who are trying to get us out."

Brown interrupted. "What about the Chetniks? Some of the guys claim they would cut off your ring finger to get the gold."

"I've heard stories the Partisans tell about the Chetniks," said George. "I don't know if this story is true, but it shows the hatred that exists between the Chetniks and Partisans. Mihailovich is playing a waiting game. For fear of reprisals the Chetniks won't fight the Germans. Because Mihailovich doesn't want Tito and the Communists in power after the war he and his men have chosen to fight the Partisans. Mihailovich, Pavelic and Tito - all three are maneuvering for political control of Yugoslavia. With the Nazi losses on many fronts, Pavelic's power is doomed. Mihailovich has already lost Allied support, so it appears Tito is in the most promising position.

"Tito has tremendous grass roots support from the people. Most of his troops are serving without pay, fighting for a better life and for freedom. Only ten percent of Tito's troops are Communists and very few of the villagers, although loyal supporters of Tito, are members of the Communist Party It'll be interesting to see who gains political power after the war."

"What about now? When will we be out of this mess?"

"As soon as we cross the last German road, which should be in another day or two."

Earlier we faced an endless number of hills and mountains. The running joke was "just over the next hill." Now our getting out was blocked by "just another German road to cross."

By late afternoon we were herded into the truck again. It was a wild ride. We were thrown from side to side as the driver sideswiped the curves and hit nearly every pothole in the road. The roads were mere trails and the wheels of the truck often became mired down in oozing mud. Then everyone climbed out to lighten the load, pushed and shoved until the truck was back on track. To make it worse, darkness had fallen making it difficult for the driver to see.

Stuck again, the driver stopped. George reported that our guide had lost his way and we would miss connections with the Partisan soldiers who were to take us across the German road. There was nothing to do but get the truck back on the road, return to the nearest town and wait until another night.

Damn these mountains! Damn the Germans! Damn the war! We were fed up with the waiting, with the filth, with the hunger, with total dependency upon others who, to us, didn't seem to know what they were doing.

Tito's Partisans in Croatia. Ivo Matusic is standing on the left.

DAY THIRTY-ONE • MONDAY • APRIL 17

I tried to scramble up the mountainside, but fell, again and again. Loose stones rolled under my feet. I couldn't get a toe-hold. German flares lit up the sky. I heard the crack of guns as bullets and shells ricocheted off the rocks. I tried over and over to climb the hill. I kept falling back. A dog barked.

I awakened with a start. Streams of sweat poured down my face. Night after night I relived the nightmare of being attacked by the Germans. Would this ordeal ever be over?

Brown joined me as we went to find our crew. Breakfast had consisted of coarse bread and the inevitable rakija. We found the men in heated conversation. With fists clenched, Reiss vented his rage. "I can't drink any more of that damned stuff. Sours my gut."

"You've been here too long."

"Too damn long. Major Jones said we'd be out of here in two days." "We'd be in Italy tonight if it hadn't been for that idiot who got us lost." "That's a lot of crap! A plane has to land first and who knows when that will be."

"Bullshit! Talking like this doesn't get us anywhere."

"Well, for Christ's sake! A guy can't complain without being shot down by the whole goddamn bunch."

More bitching. I found myself on a jagged edge. I motioned to Brown. "Let's get out of here; it's depressing enough without listening to these guys."

For security the Partisans had ordered us to stay near the barn. The town of Mazin was close by, and German sympathizers would soon find out about the large group of airmen in their town and alert the enemy. This was a good time to hit the sack. We'd be walking tonight.

At sunset we left the safety of the barn for the mountains. Even in the fading light we were touched by the beauty of the valley yellow flowers, green meadows, red-thatched barns framed on either side by wooded hills and mountains. We set off in single file, following the trail through the tall trees, gradually climbing upwards, over the saddle from the town. These mountains went on forever. We groped in the dark in silence. Up one mountain and down the other. No stopping. Our long black column inched along.

Spring rains, that nourished flowers in the valley, had covered the mountain trails with a foot of snow. The soles of our boots were heavy with the wet stuff and cold winds whipped through our flight suits. Our guides kept pushing us faster, faster. We ran up the slopes trying to match their pace, slipped and slid going down. I tripped on a snow-covered rock and fell, face first in the wet snow. Brown gave me a hand and I plodded on.

About midnight the order came to stop. Scouts reported that German troops were patrolling the area and there would be no chance of crossing the road this night. Another wild goose chase. We had walked so fast and run so hard.

DAY THIRTY-TWO • TUESDAY • APRIL 18

Our guide's call awakened us at dawn. We sensed the tension in the air as we were divided into smaller groups and quietly moved out of the barn. Sent in different directions, our bunch followed a guide to the other side of town. As we reached our designated house, we heard Partisans running and yelling, "Nimski! Nimski!" Loud bursts of gunfire exploded behind us. A shell screamed over our heads and the field in front of us literally broke into a thousand pieces. We were a dozen scared guys racing to reach the protection of the hills.

Once under cover we could take it easier, but our guide continued to climb, following the switchbacks up the mountain. Hiding behind large boulders we watched the activity below. Nazi infantry, transported in armored cars and trucks, entered the town followed by three German tanks. Shells blew up houses and other buildings near the barn where we had spent the night. We felt like animals being stalked for the kill. No matter where we were the Germans knew our position. We shuddered over our narrow escape and wondered if the others in our group were safe.

As we looked over the valley our guide pointed out where we had walked the night before. The German controlled road and railroad were on the other side of the mountain range. No vehicle could manipulate the narrow, winding trails deep with snow, but human will to survive would get us back across those mountains and give us another chance. Blasts of gunfire echoed up and down the valley. Partisans hidden among the trees fired machine guns. Their range was too short and activity too little to make real impact on the heavy shelling. I was sick at my stomach. Out-manned and under-equipped, the Partisans could not offer protection to the women and children remaining in the town.

When the firing ceased, we returned to the valley. All of us squeezed into the lean-to of a hut, seeking refuge in the place that once housed the family's animals. The farmer's wife brought us large bowls of hot polenta. Cooked without salt the porridge was tasteless, but we wolfed it down. While we were looking for hay to use as bedding, the guide burst in. He motioned wildly with his arms, shouting "Nimski! Nimski!"

Under cover of darkness we silently slipped out of the lean-to and followed him up the mountain and across the first saddle. We finally reached a cluster of huts. Numb with fatigue we threw ourselves down on a dirt floor and fell asleep.

DAY THIRTY-THREE • WEDNESDAY • APRIL 19

We awoke to sounds of cattle. No signs nor sounds of war. Cows and a few calves were grazing on the hillside.

By the time we were up and out, the sun was high in the sky. A teen-age girl brought us large pitchers of milk, several loaves of coarse, dark bread, and the biggest surprise, home-churned butter. A feast for kings! We tore the bread apart and smothered the pieces with fresh, sweet butter. The best treat was the milk, cool and sweet. I gulped it down. The young girl filled my cup again. This was only the second time I'd been offered milk since we were shot down.

Frustrated as we were with the delay, we enjoyed a day of rest in this peaceful village, isolated from fear, from shooting and killing. By late afternoon the order came to move. We walked several hours, backtracking to a village near the valley. Some of our downhill route was a narrow road, formed by sheep and cattle taken to the mountains for summer grazing.

A Yugoslav major met us in the village. Speaking in German he told us he would be guiding us across the German held road.

DAY THIRTY-FOUR • THURSDAY • APRIL 20

Although we never knew what direction we were going, we could re-trace our steps by the towns we remembered. Returning to Mazin the next morning we were glad to see the other fellows. We learned that one man had been captured by the Germans and another killed by a bullet during the fighting.

Later we heard the details. George Morrell, copilot on a Liberator, was the man who had been killed. When the fighting started Lt. Fred Streicher and his group started racing for cover in the nearby hills. Looking back, Morrell saw that his pilot, Streicher, had been hit by gunfire. Running over to help, he noticed that his pilot's leg was partially severed and bleeding profusely. He took off his belt to use as a tourniquet, and as he was tying it around Streicher's leg Morrell was surrounded by German soldiers. After beating Streicher, the soldiers shot Morrell and left both men lying on the ground. In a short time two German officers arrived and found that Morrell was dead. Streicher, although unconscious, was still alive. They dressed Streicher in Morrell's clothes, took him prisoner and left his companion lying on the ground. It was the Partisans who found Morrell's body and buried him on the mountainside. Our rescue had seemed so near, but for Morrell, that time would never come.

Walking about the town we crossed deep tracks formed by the tanks and motorcycles and saw the destruction. Houses were burned or destroyed. Shops were in shambles. A few villagers were pawing through the rubble, trying to find parts of their possessions to help rebuild their lives. Others were sweeping up the debris, carrying it away in wheelbarrows. The Germans had taken most of the food and seized twenty men and women to use as forced labor. I was thankful that our families at home were not experiencing the horrors of war: homes burned, food and animals seized, people tortured and killed. In Yugoslavia, the war touched everyone — civilians and soldiers alike.

Although we felt uneasy about staying in Mazin, we were forced to wait for the Major. By late afternoon he came with about twenty soldiers from his battalion. Their presence was proof that crossing the German road wouldn't be easy. With the last rays of sunlight, we started for the mountains. The Major and twelve of his men had left two hours earlier to check the route. For several hours we walked the mountain trails, muddy from melting snow. Only with thorough knowledge of the terrain could the soldiers find their way in the blackness of the night.

Near the bottom of a steep hill we encountered a rocky gorge. Slipping and sliding we worked our way down the rock face of the ravine, stopping from time to time to listen. Someplace beneath us lay the railroad and German patrols.

When we heard the clatter of the Partisans' hobnailed shoes on the cobbled streets, we knew we had reached a town. Leaving the road, we walked stealthily around houses and sneaked across yards and gardens. As if to let us know they were watching our every move, the Germans fired a parachute flare. The area lit up briefly, showing the railroad running parallel to the major road.

Standing in the clammy mist one hundred paces above the road, we watched German patrols come and go. After one group had entered the patrol hut, fresh smoke would rise from the chimney. Then a relief patrol would come out and start down the road.

Once again, we were divided into groups, the Partisan soldiers interspersed among us. The point of crossing was to be only 500 yards from the patrol house. As each group was given the signal to leave, the whispered call came down the column, "Otstojanje," or "ten paces between each man." Crouching low we skimmed the tracks, then raced down and over the road.

We made it! We had crossed the last hurdle... Alive.

Now to stay alive.

DAY THIRTY-FIVE • FRIDAY • APRIL 21

As we approached a cluster of cottages, we expected the Partisans to stop and rest. Afraid the Germans might be patrolling the area our guides pressed on. We were exhausted. Even walking on the level ground in the valley was an effort. The night's trek had sapped our energy.

At dawn the guides stopped for a few hours, but by ten o'clock we were walking again, trekking up and down the wooded hills. By afternoon we reached a village called Boboljuske.

With no food since the evening before, my mind was set on one thing, getting something to eat. Spotting a group under a large oak tree, I joined them and found women serving soup out of an iron pot. Loaves of fresh-baked black bread were stacked on the ground. We tore apart the bread and along with it gulped down a bowl of watery soup. Looking at the large pot, I wondered if it held seconds. When Gordon held up his bowl for more, the woman looked at him with a shocked expression. She shook her ladle at him, as if to say, "Don't you appreciate what we've given you?" We wondered how they could consider this meager meal as adequate.

The Yugoslav major motioned for us to follow him. He had found good barns for sleeping. With clean hay for bedding we were in lively spirits and made bets on when we'd be in Italy. But my thoughts returned to food. Visions of juicy peaches, stacks of pancakes dripping with syrup and melted butter, a double-dipper ice-cream cone. When would we get some real food?

DAY THIRTY-SIX • SATURDAY • APRIL 22

Spring could be beautiful in Yugoslavia. Blue sky, bright sunshine, the scent of flowering bushes in the air. A range of hills rose in the distance. Following our guides up and down the rolling hills we had a view of the wide green valley surrounding the Una River. Walking during daylight in the open country was an unusual experience for us. Women were working in the fields, pushing heavy wooden plows through the brown soil. It was planting time.

The terrain changed. Walking single file, we hiked through forests of oaks and beeches, forded a couple of streams, and sloshed through the muddy knee-deep water. Crossing a railroad that had been blown up, the Partisan guides indicated this was their work. Sabotaging railroads was a quick and effective way of disrupting movement of German troops and supplies.

Rumors traveled up and down the line that our next stop would be Tito's headquarters. Perhaps we would see the great man himself. Approaching the town, we noticed tire tracks in the muddy road. They looked like tracks from an American jeep. As we came closer the valley narrowed and a range of hills rose abruptly, forming high cliffs on either side above the river. Between us and the hills lay the town of Drvar.

We walked into Drvar, a bunch of half-starved airmen wearing filthy flight suits and mud-caked boots. This town, too, showed the ravages of war. The enemy had left its signature in the gutted houses clustered around the ruins of what had once been a furniture factory.

Finding food was always top priority, and in Drvar we were not disappointed. Food supplies had been dropped by Allied planes along with medicine, ammunition, boots, and other materials needed by the Partisan army. At the Communist headquarters we saw hundreds and hundreds of cans of K rations. We were allowed a choice of breakfast, lunch or dinner and each allotted a can and a half. One of the officer's aides served us English tea, refilling our cups several times. We were in a daze. We felt sorry for the infantry who often depended upon K-rations. No more. This was more food than we had seen in weeks. Staying in Drvar for a few days didn't look so bad.

DAY THIRTY-SEVEN • SUNDAY • APRIL 23

In the morning we walked around the town, wondering why the commander of the Partisan Army had chosen this site for the 5th Corps Headquarters, a place where even planes could not land. George explained that when the front changed, Tito was forced to move. Near the Una River was a large cave. It was here Tito had set up his private quarters, a place the enemy would not easily suspect.

Historically, there were other reasons for Tito to choose Drvar for his hideout. Located in western Bosnia, Drvar had been a Croatian military frontier against the Turks in the sixteenth century. Before the present war, the town, with its saw mills, was the center of a timber industry. The workers had formed the first local Partisan units in Bosnia and had gone underground before the Germans occupied the country.

We headed for the Communist headquarters to see if anyone had the scoop on getting back to Italy. As we entered the building we were introduced to several British and American liaison officers assigned to Tito's Headquarters. Colonel Randolph Churchill, sent by his father, Winston Churchill, was the VIP of the group. Captain Lynn Farish and his aide from the U.S. parachuted in with radio equipment and were in charge of sending communications back to the Allies. We pestered the officers with questions.

"When would planes be coming to take us out?"

"Where would they land?"

"Would they be C-47's as Major Jones said?"

Noticing the steep cliffs and hills around Drvar we wondered where any plane could land.

Captain Farish told us that Lt. Colonel Neveleff had come by plane from Bari the week before and spent several days in Drvar, meeting with Tito and preparing the groundwork for evacuating us. We would be flown out on C-47s that brought supplies to the Partisans. Instead of dropping supplies by parachute, the pilot would land the plane, unload the supplies, and we would be his return cargo. Weather was a determining factor, so they never knew in advance when planes would arrive. Bari was only two hours by plane from the airstrip, a half-day's walk from Drvar. I thought to myself, "So near — and yet so far."

Sharp, well-pressed uniforms and polished shoes that at one time snapped me to attention, no longer ruled my actions. This time I felt no embarrassment visiting with the clean-shaven Farish and the other officers. I had quit worrying about my appearance long ago. Other factors were more important than neat uniforms.

111

Simple things in life, often taken for granted, became significant. Things like a square meal, a shower, clean clothes with no lice, a bed safe from strafing, seeing family again — and just being alive.

Once again pilots were asked to give the names of their crews, so they could be radioed back to Air Corps Headquarters in Bari. While writing down the names and serial numbers, I heard Brown call me. A jeep was being driven down the street with Marshall Tito in the front seat. I dashed out, but by the time I reached the rest of our guys, the jeep had passed. You win some and lose some. At least someday I could tell my grandchildren that I saw the back of Tito's head!

DAY THIRTY-EIGHT • MONDAY • APRIL 24

Since the airstrip was a half day's walk from Drvar we left town early in the morning. After climbing the steep hills above the Una Valley, we found the view spectacular: A high peak towered to the right and mountains stretched far in the distance behind us. Snow was still on the highest hills, but in the valley the sun was hot. We passed an old woman leading a pony laden with hay. As she walked, she was singing, probably an old Bosnian folk song. We were ever amazed at the optimistic, cheerful spirit shown by the Yugoslavs, young and old alike.

Walking made us thirsty and from time to time we stopped to drink from a mountain stream. The trail took us up a steep cliff, across a stretch of open meadow and another climb into thick pine forests. By afternoon we came out of the dense woods and overlooked a large flat area. Pointing, our guides said, "Petrovac Polje." So, this was the place we had walked so far to reach, an immense grassland surrounded by mountains.

Smoke rising from chimneys gave evidence of a small village. The tower of a mosque jutted above the white roofs in the town. It was here we were to be picked up one of these nights by a plane flying in from Italy, that is if the Germans didn't find the landing strip before we had a chance to get out.

DAY THIRTY-NINE • TUESDAY • APRIL 25

At dawn I was awakened by the deafening roar of planes flying over the town. I panicked. These must be the C-47s arriving to take us to Italy and we wouldn't make it to the airstrip in time. Gordon and Spoon ran into the barn, shouting that the two planes were Stukas. The Germans had tracked us down again. We should have known better than to think a large, flat, grassland area in the middle of Yugoslavia could be kept a secret from the Germans.

We went outside. There was no mistaking those tilted wings and the wasp-like undercarriage. The Stuka was little threat in other theaters of the war, but in Yugoslavia, without antiaircraft defenses, it had retained all its old terror. One of the pilots took his preliminary run high, but immediately turned back and came screaming downwards, bombs crashing on grassland outside the town. As quickly as the planes appeared, they were gone, and silence followed, broken only by shouts for help and the crying of frightened children.

The town of Bosan Petrovac lay on the edge of one of the few stretches of flat grassland in the highlands of Bosnia. On the far side, perhaps five or six miles away, was a range of mountains. Several months before we arrived, land had been leveled for an airstrip near Petrovac and used by the British Royal Air Force to bring in a steady flow of materials and supplies for the Partisans. It was strategically located so that military supplies could be distributed to the divisions and brigades in Croatia, Slovenia, and Bosnia.

Most of the time the airstrip was to receive supplies dropped by parachutes during the night. But when airmen or wounded Partisans needed transportation to Italy, the pilot risked a landing, if weather conditions permitted, and flew them back to Bari.

To coordinate the war efforts between Tito's Partisans and the Allied command in Italy and North Africa, men volunteered to parachute into Yugoslavia with radio wireless equipment. Captain Lynn Farish was such a man. He and his aide maintained radio communications with Bari and North Africa. Reports were sent to headquarters on the military situation in Yugoslavia. Names of Allied airmen, their serial numbers, and the date of their landing in Yugoslavia were included.

Communicating weather conditions from the Balkans to Italy was essential for scheduling Allied bombing missions in Rumania, Bulgaria and the Balkan Peninsula. Requests for guns and ammunition, food and medical supplies for Tito's troops were also relayed to Bari. In turn, commanding officers with the 97th

Bomb Group suggested specific targets or enemy lines of communication to be sabotaged by the Partisans.

To protect the airstrip, planes flew in only at night and activity during the day was camouflaged by laborers working the fields nearby. A headquarters had been established in the town for organizing the operation. They informed the 15th Air Force in Bari about the supplies needed by Partisans and the number of airmen and wounded Partisan soldiers waiting to be flown out.

As for food, K-rations were supplemented with British rations including canned butter and sugar. Wherever there were British there was tea, and they had even requisitioned Carnation cream to add to their tea. After existing on straw bread and watery soup for five weeks, such luxuries seemed extravagant.

Our thoughts and conversation focused on the arrival of a plane from Bari. The meteorologist reported that a storm was brewing over the Adriatic which meant no planes this night.[8]

---

[8] Weather reports are crucial for flying. The Yugoslav Partisans provided this vital information.

DAY FORTY • WEDNESDAY • APRIL 26

"Rise and Shine, Stuka time." Brown was shaking me and shouting the alert. It was 0600. Planes rumbled overhead. It was obvious the Germans knew about the airstrip and the supplies being dropped by Allied planes at night. Two Stukas swooped down, circled the town and plastered a field nearby with a volley of bombs. It never left my mind that Yugoslav family members as well as Partisans were being killed, and that we could be next.

Weather had improved, and it was rumored that tonight a plane would be coming in to take us out. We walked to the airstrip with people from the village. Kneeling, as if we were planting potatoes, we checked the runway for stones or any litter which could damage the planes. We filled holes with dirt. A hundred or more people held hands, walking back and forth over the length of the runway, trampling down the grass. When we had cleaned the field, it looked like pasture land.

"Where's the gas for the planes?" I asked the British officer.

"Gas and oil supplies are hidden underground. The Partisans are masters at camouflage."

Gordon stepped up. "Do the planes carry guns in case they're attacked?"

"No. But even though the pilot and copilot fly in unarmed C-47s, the greatest risk is landing planes at night in this mountainous country. They can't use landing lights."

Toward midnight we walked to the airstrip again. Stars were out, and we were confident this would be our lucky night. The Partisans had a system of priorities for flying people out. The sick and wounded went first followed by evadees who had been here the longest. No one in the group had parachuted into the country earlier than our crew, so leaving on the plane was almost assured for us.

We settled down on the cold ground to wait, holding oil-soaked rags to be lit if a plane arrived. Excitement was in the air. In a short time, we heard the drone of engines. As the plane circled overhead, the Partisans shot flares to identify the aircraft. Even though the Germans had been strafing at dawn, we couldn't assume a plane coming in at night would be ours.

Watching eagerly, we shouted almost in unison, "It's a C-47!" When the British colonel gave the signal, we lay down on the airstrip to guide the pilot. The plane came nearer, circling yet again. We were waiting for the pilot to make his approach for a landing. He made another pass, and then turned toward the hills. Near the town several parachutes could be seen.

In the span of a few minutes the pilot circled above us, dropped his cargo then flew away into the night, leaving us bewildered and confused,

Silence was broken by the Partisans who started running to find the parachutes. Their primary interest was unpacking the supplies: ammunition, guns, medicines, and food. They worked in the dark, piling the dropped cargo into heavy carts or kolas hitched to ponies. Supplies were taken into town to be distributed. For a time, this had been done by day, but soon the Germans discovered what was happening. Receiving news of a drop they would send aircraft to patrol all the tracks leading away from Bosan Petrovak. After several caravans had been shot up by day, the Partisans transported supplies only at night.

Guns and ammunition were essential to fight a war. These items were greatly appreciated and protected carefully. They even turned the bags inside out, to see if any items had been missed. This last frantic search was, we learned, for the one item they wanted most. American cigarettes!

Walking slowly back to the village I prayed that tomorrow night a plane would land and take us out. Every day we had prayed for escape. Reiss said his Hail Marys and the rest of us talked to God in our own way. Would our prayers ever be answered?

DAY FORTY-ONE • THURSDAY • APRIL 27

The Stukas were back again, as regular as a clock. Another day. More joshing. These long, anxious days were taking their toll. What about the plane that didn't land? Did the pilot chicken out, or didn't he know that eighty, weary, starving men had been trying for forty days to reach the Allies and safety?

Close to midnight we walked again to the airstrip. Surely tonight the planes would come. Signal fires were lit and once more we sat down to wait. Time passed slowly. Several fellows fell asleep. Others described their first meal in detail, and what they would do when they got to Italy. Most of us were looking forward to a leave for home. The fires had gone out, but we continued to wait, telling each other to be quiet so we could hear the plane.

The Partisans, too, were restless. The weather was good, so there seemed to be no reason for cancelling the flight. Captain Farish reminded them that good weather in the Balkans didn't necessarily mean that meteorological conditions were good in Italy.

After almost six weeks, we had had plenty of time to practice patience, but somehow these days were the longest ones of all. Finally, we got up, stiff from sitting on the cold, damp ground. No plane would be coming tonight.

DAY FORTY-TWO • FRIDAY • APRIL 28

As we were eating our breakfast of black bread and tea, Curry came by with the news. Awakening early, he got the scoop from George. A Russian plane had landed a couple of hours after we left the airstrip last night. The British sergeant who waited at the field saw the plane circling the area for half an hour. Near daylight the pilot approached the field to land. The engines stalled, and the plane dropped about thirty feet straight down onto the runway, damaging its landing gear. Rumor was that the pilot had plenty of Vodka on board.

As the pilot climbed out of the plane, the British sergeant cussed him up and down for landing in daylight. German pilots could spot the Russian plane and bomb the airfield, putting it out of use for days. Since the plane could not be flown out, the sergeant found Partisans who dismantled it in short order.

More bad news followed. Gordon had a high fever and was vomiting. He needed to get back to Italy — and soon. Others in our party had dysentery, and to top it off in early evening, nine critically wounded Partisan soldiers were brought in to be transported to Italy for hospitalization. The sick and wounded would be the first on the plane. Our chances of getting out soon were diminishing fast.

Again, we took our midnight walk to the airstrip. Captain Farish said at least one plane was scheduled to arrive. Those who were able, carried the sick and wounded on makeshift stretchers. Once again, we waited. And, once again… no plane.

Curry reminded us of the day's good news. This had been the first morning the German Stukas hadn't strafed the town. If they had seen the Russian plane, the airstrip would have been bombed. An Angel of God was looking over us!

DAY FORTY-THREE • SATURDAY • APRIL 29

Rise and shine... Stuka time!

At 0600, the Germans were back on schedule, strafing the town and countryside. In the five days we had been in Petrovak, we'd been visited by plenty of German planes, but not one Allied plane had landed here. We wondered if planes had ever landed at Petrovak. Our spirits sagged. Counting the sick and wounded, there were about ninety men waiting for transportation. This meant we needed not one plane but several. Prospects for getting out looked dim.

I finally found Captain Parish to express my concerns about Gordon, who needed medical care immediately. He assured me radio contact had been made with Bari each day and every attempt was being made for a plane to reach us. I prayed to God that a flight would come in time.

We walked to the airstrip at night, once again carrying the sick on stretchers. We sat on the ground, straining our ears for the drone of American engines. Our mood was upbeat. Suddenly a dead silence interrupted the chattering and laughter. Without a doubt we heard an airplane. In the blackness the plane began to circle lower and lower through the clouds, over the *polje* towards the improvised runway. We started to move the badly wounded Partisans, bringing them as near the landing strip as possible.

As the pilot approached the field, forty of us lay down on either side of the runway holding flaming oil-soaked rags in our outstretched hands. Guided by the light of our flares, the pilot made his approach and landed the plane as we drew back to give him room.

As soon as the door of the plane opened, the guys formed a line, handing the boxes of supplies from one to another. Spoon and I rushed over to pick up Gordon and hoisted him into the plane. Saying "Good-bye," we assured him we'd see him soon in Bari. Our words sounded more hopeful than the present situation justified.

After other airmen had squeezed in with the sick and wounded, the doors were shut and the pilot, who had kept his engines running, maneuvered the plane into position for takeoff. In minutes the plane was airborne on its way back to Italy. Although we were left to wait until another night, we knew the system was working.

DAY FORTY-FOUR • SUNDAY • APRIL 30

This was still the fourth month of '44. Today was the forty-fourth day since we parachuted into Yugoslavia. Would this be our lucky day?

By evening a chill wind whipped around the *polje* and clouds concealed the stars. It was a cold walk to the airstrip. The Partisans prepared the signal fires, hoping the planes could get under the cloud cover. Conversation was muffled as we strained to hear the sound of engines.

About midnight we heard one! For five minutes its engines droned in the blackness. Each time the sound grew louder we grabbed our oil-soaked rags, ready to lie down on the field when the plane appeared.

Gradually the sound became faint and finally was no longer audible. We figured the pilot was not willing to chance a landing with the low cloud cover. With these mountains and the Germans so close we marveled that anyone would risk his life to save us. But recognizing the reason for the pilot's decision didn't help our morale. Once again, we walked back to the village, — discouraged, disgruntled, disappointed.

DAY FORTY-FIVE • MONDAY • MAY 1

As usual, we were awakened by the Stukas making their early morning call. It was hard to understand why the Germans were wasting their bombs on this isolated village. Fortunately, few had been killed and the airstrip was still unharmed.

Today was May Day. A year ago, I was at Blytheville, Arkansas, flying AT-9s and looking forward to receiving my wings. That day seemed light years away. Combat had changed me, had changed all of us. I was anxious to get back in the cockpit and fly again, but the glamour of being a bomber pilot was tarnished. I saw firsthand the devastation and misery caused by war.

About 2300 we left the barn to walk to the airstrip. There were grumblings and complaints from many of the men. We sat on the cold ground looking up at the stars, waiting and hoping to hear a familiar drone of American engines. I checked my watch. It was after midnight.

We had almost given up hope when we heard the sound, first faint, then louder. Once again, the Partisans shot flares for identification. As the plane became visible, cheers rang out, "It's ours! It's a C-47!"

We hurried to light our oil-soaked rags and lay down on the ground to guide the pilot onto the makeshift runway. As if to test our patience, the pilot circled the field two times before making the approach for landing. Holding onto my homemade flare, I watched the plane as it touched down, its wheels bumping over the uneven surface of the grass until it came to a stop. When the pilot and copilot stepped down, they were greeted with cheers and rebel yells. Looking at us, they must have wondered how these dirty, emaciated airmen had managed to survive. Our tattered Air Force uniforms were supplemented with bits of native garb. Spoon was still sporting his Daniel Boone cap.

While the engines were running, we helped unload the supplies, handing them from one man to the next. We figured we were being paid by the head. Thinking of the courage it took to fly into a mountainous country at night Reiss said to the pilot, "If **I** were in Italy and **you** were in Yugoslavia, I wouldn't risk my butt to come and get you."

"Damn-it, get on the plane," growled the pilot. "We're running late."

Quickly we scrambled inside, enlisted men followed by the officers. The doors were shut, the engines roared, and we jolted over the ground for the take-off. Another few seconds and we were airborne. For weeks we had been waiting for this moment.

There were no seats. We sat on the floor, about forty of us jammed into the body of a C-47. As usual, Reiss's voice could be heard above the others.

"I promised myself faithfully, if God ever got me out of that mess down there, I would **never, ever** get in another airplane. And here I am, flying in this old crate — and without a parachute to boot!"

I, too, had made a promise. I bowed my head and gave thanks to God. The words of the Psalmist came to my mind —

"Yea, though I walk through the valley of the shadow of death,

I will fear no evil; for thou art with me."

God had not deserted us. He had been our "Copilot" all the way.

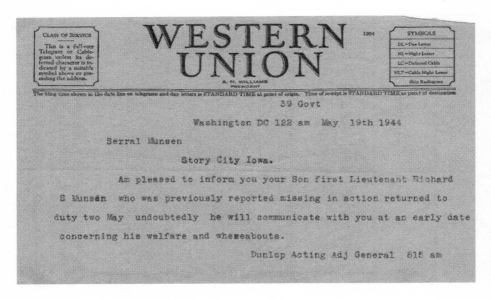

The crew of B-17 #472 flew out of Bosan Petrovac, Bosnia, the night of May 1/2. While en route to the States, Dick cabled his parents from Casablanca to inform them of his safety. On his arrival in New York on May 14, he visited with them by telephone. On May 19 his parents drove to Ames to meet Dick at the train station. When they arrived back in Story City the above telegram from the War Department was in the door.

BIOGRAPHICAL DATA

OF

CREW MEMBERS

**FIRST LIEUTENANT
RICHARD MUNSEN, PILOT
Age 22**

Born in Story City, IA, on December 1, 1921, Dick was six years old when Lindbergh made his non-stop slight across the Atlantic. The son of an automobile dealer, he was more interested in cars than planes. In the summers Dick washed cars and did custodial chores and later took his turn as parts man, bookkeeper, and car salesman. After graduation from Story City High School, he worked for his father one year and continued working part-time for two years while commuting to Iowa State College, majoring in engineering.

In September 1942 he enlisted in the Army Air Force. He made his first training flight on November 24th and received his wings on May 28, 1943. After completing B-17 Combat School, he was sent to Pyote TX where Cletus Reiss, Calvin Churchill, Cecil Sullivant, Harley Spoon and Paul Marion joined his crew. They were reassigned to Alexandria LA for two moths of Intensive Combat Training. Irv Williamson, Sanford Plautz, Harold Shapiro, and Vern Curry completed the roster. On the second anniversary of Pearl Harbor, Dick and his crew left Morrison Field FL to fly combat missions with the 15th Air Force in Italy. He was awarded the Distinguished Flying Cross and Purple Heart.

Upon Dick's return to the air base at Amendola, Italy on May 4, he was granted a leave to the States and flew to New York via Casablanca and the Azores. In September 1944 Dick married his high school girlfriend, Katherine (Kay) Jacobson. He attended engineering school at Chanute Field, IL in the fall and winter of 1944-45 and was prepared to supervise a sub depot for B-29s in the Far East when the war with Japan ended. He was discharged as a captain.

After the war Dick returned to his hometown where he became a partner with his father in the Munsen Chevrolet-Buick agency. He was a dealer for forty-five years before his retirement.

Dick and Kay have five children: Richard, Jr., Anne Marie, Sylvia, Paul, and Craig. They have three grandsons, and one great grandson.

Dick was the last surviving member of the crew of #472 and lived 96 wonderful years. He passed peacefully on February 5, 2018.

Kay now resides in Tucson AZ and still writing. She also authored **23 Lessons** that chronicles Dick's pilot training the 22 missions prior to being shot down.

SEARGEANT ROBERT BROWN
WAIST GUNNER – AGE 20

Robert Brown, the oldest of four boys, grew up in Rensselaer IN. After graduation from high school, Bob worked at the Kingsbury Ordinance Plant in the distribution division where 20mm shells were assembled and loaded.

Knowing he would be drafted, Bob enlisted in the V-5 Program at Ball State Teachers College as a Naval Cadet. His navy career was cut short. While doing stalls and spins on a regular training flight, it started to snow heavily. He temporarily lost his bearings and landed the plane in a farmer's field. After receiving directions, he flew back to the airport. All was well until he told his roommate. When the word reached the board, he was given the option of staying in the Navy in a non-flying capacity or being discharged. Dismissed in late January 1943, he enlisted in the Army Air Forces March 5.

After basic training, Bob attended gunnery and armament schools. Assigned to the 772nd Squadron in the 463rd Bomb Group, he trained with his B-17 crew in South Dakota and Florida. On February 14, 1944, he left the States by the southern route and arrived at Amendola, Italy, on March 14. Like all new men arriving from the States, Bob was assigned to an experienced crew on his first mission. His claim to fame is having one of the shortest tours of duty at Amendola – four days. Bob's diary, written on the scene, provided invaluable information for reconstructing the men's long trek through Yugoslavia.

Bob arrived in New York City on May 14, Mother's Day. When he called home, his parents wept. They knew he was missing and had assumed he was killed. The telegram informing them of Bob's safety did not arrive until May 19. After a furlough at home, Bob was stationed at Chanute Field, close enough to continue the courtship of his high school girlfriend, Charlotte Ann Nesius. They were married February 1, 1945. Bob attended Purdue University for three semesters. When a position became available at the Rensselaer Post Office, Bob was offered the job and remained there for thirty years.

Bob and Charlotte reared four sons, Bob Jr., Bill, Pat and Mike (twins) and 11 grandchildren. After retirement in 1979, Bob and Charlotte divided their time between Rensselaer and Naples, Florida.

Bob remained one of Dick's closest friends, for 68 years. Bob left us on September 1, 2012.

SERGEANT VERN CURRY
TAIL GUNNER

Vern Curry worked at the Rock Island Illinois Arsenal after attending high school in Muscatine, Iowa. Feeling it was his patriotic duty to enter the military Vern enlisted in the Air Force on October 28, 1942. After completing twenty weeks of Mechanics School, he volunteered for gunnery training because he wanted to see action overseas. Vern joined Dick's crew at Alexandria in September 1943. Quiet, patient, and a little shy, the other men in the crew found him friendly and likable.

Assigned to the ball turret, Vern was not happy with that vulnerable spot. When Cletus Reiss volunteered to fly in the ball, Vern took the tail position. Handling a .50 caliber gun on a B-17 was a job Vern knew he was trained to do. He flew 21 missions and was credited with shooting down a Focke-Wulf 190 when the plane was attacked near Udine. Vern was never afraid when flying missions but being shot down was scary. He chose to block out most of his experiences in Yugoslavia, but the crew reunions brought back many memories. He was awarded the Air Medal with two bronze clusters, Purple Heart and Silver Star. One of ten children, Vern and three of his four brothers fought in World War II.

After returning to the States, Vern was an instructor in Gunnery School until discharged in October 1945. He returned to Muscatine and met Ruth through a mutual friend. They were married April 1, 1946. After driving a tank truck for Peters Oil Company for ten years, Vern joined his brother-in-law in the feed and grain business.

Vern and Ruth have four children, Connie, Steve, Sam and Scott, and eight grandchildren. With all the children living in Muscatine, theirs is a close-knit family. They enjoy family dinners and taking vacations together. After Vern's retirement in 1987, he and Ruth traveled throughout the United States.

Vern passed away on July 20, 2006.

**SERGEANT CLETUS REISS
BALL TURRET GUNNER**

Cletus Moses Reiss was born on May 21, 1923 in Ramsey IL. A star football player in the Assumption IL High School, Cletus Reiss was a big fellow to ride in a ball turret on a B-17. But by wearing an electric flight suit he managed to squeeze into the cramped quarters.

Cletus won a football scholarship but left college in January 1943 to enlist in the Army Air Force. An independent and practical fellow, Cletus rebelled at the duties imposed in basic training. He complained to the base Commander that freedom from "that kind of crap" was what the war was all about. Turning down a chance to go to Officers' Training, he was sent to gunnery school. Cletus prided himself on being able to take a .50 caliber gun apart and put it together again blind folded, with gloves on. Comfortable with guns, he was shy around girls. Cletus joined Dick's crew at the infamous "Rattlesnake Base" in Pyote, Texas.

Eleven months after entering the Air Force, Cletus was on his way overseas. During one of his 21 missions the mechanism in the ball turret malfunctioned and Dick was forced to land the plane with Cletus riding in the ball — an anxious time for all the crew. He was awarded the Silver Star for that mission. He also received the Purple Heart and Air Medal with two bronze clusters. While making the trek through Yugoslavia, Cletus wondered who was caring for the pet monkey he had bought in Brazil before taking off on the long hop to Africa.

When he was overseas, Cletus received letters from a pen pal named Rieta. Returning to the States in May of '44, Cletus looked up Rieta and it was love at first sight. They were married On November 19, 1944. He joined Korschot's Heating & Air Conditioning in Lafayette IN. During his forty years with the company, Cletus helped them become the largest dealer in the area.

Cletus and Rieta have four sons, Lane, Dale, Dennis, and Gene, and six grandchildren. Reflecting on his experiences in Yugoslavia he wrote, "I wouldn't do it again for a million, and darn near wouldn't take that amount for it not to have happened."

Cletus passed away on January 17, 2016.

LIEUTENANT L. BAILEY GORDON
COPILOT

Except for his years in the military, Bailey Gordon lived all his life in Dallas TX. On January 26, 1942, while attending North Texas Agricultural College, he joined the Army Aviation Cadets. He was 20 years old when he received his wings on November 10, 1942.

Bailey was assigned to Fighter Tactical School in Florida and flew P-39s. He went by boat to North Africa in early 1943 and joined the 154 Tactical Reconnaissance Squadron, flying P-39s, P-51s, and P-38s. In mid-January Bailey's squadron was moved to Bari. Since there was little need for his squadron in Italy, pilots were given a chance to transfer to other aircraft.

Figuring they could fly their required missions quickly, be promoted, and return to the States in a short time, Bailey and nine other pilots chose four-engine bombers. They hadn't been told the other side of the story. Losses of men and planes had been considerable during the winter of '44 so four-engine requests were readily granted.

Gordon and his P-39 buddies reported to the 97th Bomb Group at Amendola the middle of February, were issued tents, and saw a B-17 for the first time. After ten hours of four-engine training they were sent into combat as copilots. The target of Gordon's first mission on February 23rd was a ball bearing factory in Steyr, Austria. His plane encountered intense flak and rocket fire from scores of German fighters. Gordon's initiation into the air war in Italy was a baptism of fire. He was awarded the Purple Heart, Presidential Citation Medal, and Air Medal.

After returning to the States in May 1944, Bailey thought a story should be written about his experiences. He dictated everything he could remember to a friend, who filled 23 typewritten pages with his story. The many references to specific foods, available or not available, indicate that food was always on the minds of the men. It is the detail included in Bailey's record that proved invaluable in writing the men's story.

In June of 1944, Bailey married Martha Sue Dabney. After receiving his discharge in October 1945 Bailey continued flying for 32 years with Pioneer Airlines, Texas International Airlines, and Continental Airlines. He retired in October 1982. Bailey and Sue have three children, Bob, Susan and Martye, and four grandchildren.

Bailey died on February 20, 2007.

COPILOT
LIEUTENANT IRVIN WILLIAMSON

Irv Williamson grew up in Michigan. He joined Dick's crew in Alexandria LA. Always interested in photography, he took pictures of the crew on the base at Amendola, Italy, and in the plane while flying a mission. Irv and his wife, Frankie, had three children and lived in Vancouver, WA. Irv died on August 28, 1995.

ENGINEER
STAFF SERGEANT HARLEY SPOON

A competent and dependable flight engineer, Harley Spoon made the Army Air Force his career, serving in the Pacific as well as in the European theater of war. He died in 1989.

LEFT WAIST GUNNER
SERGEANT CECIL SULLIVANT

Any man over the age of 30 in the Air Force was an "old man," and so Sully was often called Pop by the crew. He returned to his home town of Memphis TN after the war. Sully died March 25, 1979.

NAVIGATOR
LIEUTENANT WILLIAM SEWARD

On March 18, Bill Seward was flying his first mission with the crew of ship #472. Efforts to contact him have been unsuccessful.

RADIO OPERATOR
SERGEANT PAUL MARION

A native of Archbald, Pennsylvania, Paul attended Penn State University for one semester before enlisting in the Army Air Force in June 1942. He attended the Air Force Radio Operator's School in Sioux Falls SD and Gunnery School at Pensacola FL. He joined the crew at Pyote TX.

Paul was the only member of the crew to fall into unfriendly hands after bailing out. He was turned over to the Germans and spent thirteen months as a Prisoner of War.

After his discharge from the service, he met and married Betty Reap. He resumed his education at George Washington University, graduating from the University School of Government with a major in accounting. He worked as an auditor with the U.S. General Accounting Office in Washington, D.C. and Europe, as Director of Auditing of the Economic Development administration, and later as Director of Internal Audits for the Department of Health, Education, and Welfare. He retired from this position in 1978.

Since retirement Paul and Betty divided their time between Clearwater FL and Ocean City MD. They have one son, Frank.

PAUL MARION – PRISONER OF WAR

Parachuting into enemy held territory in time of war was a risky business. Landing sites were chosen by the German fighters. Hanging by ropes from immense white chutes, the men were easy targets and their positions radioed by fighter pilots to German headquarters on the ground. Fortunately for the crew of B-17 #472, the chutes were also seen by the Partisans who searched the mountainous areas for the men. Landing close to the northern coast of the Adriatic, Germans fortifications were strong. The men could have been picked up by friend or foe. Paul Marion, radio operator, was the only one of the crew to fall into enemy hands and taken prisoner. But for the Grace of God the other men could have suffered the same plight. Paul Marion tells his story.

When we parachuted into Yugoslavia, I landed in a ravine. I covered my parachute with snow and climbed half way up the ravine where there was considerable shrubbery. I hid there most of the day and saw several patrols of soldiers walking through the ravine. (To this day, I wonder if they were the group that helped the others find their way back.) In any event, towards nightfall I climbed to the top of the ravine to try to better orient myself to the surrounding area. At this point, I encountered a patrol of Yugoslavian soldiers. They all wore red stars, supposedly the badge of Tito's Partisans, so initially I thought I was in friendly hands. They took me and two other Americans they had previously picked up to a barracks in the area. I injured my elbows in the jump and was in some pain. They bandaged my elbows and gave each of us a bottle of cold wine. We spent the night there.

The next morning, they marched us to Trieste and turned us over to the Germans. The Germans put us in individual cells in what, I presume, was the city jail. We spent about three days there and I had an excellent, ground level view from my cell window of an Allied bombing raid.

After three days, we walked, under guard, through the city to the railroad station. This trip was made eventful by the civilians we encountered. They shouted at us and a few threw vegetables at us. We boarded a train and spent the better part of the day traveling to a facility, which I later learned was an interrogation center for POWs. I spent about one week at this center. While there I was locked in a wooden cubicle about 3 feet by 7 feet — just about enough room for a cot. It was windowless. I was taken from my room about every other day for interrogation. This usually consisted of threats of execution or corporal punishment.

After a week or so of this, I was taken, together with the other two Americans who were captured with me, by train to a POW camp called "Barth" in Northwest Germany. It was a camp for English officers. Apparently, the German guards who accompanied us delivered us to Barth by mistake. They were literally given "hell" by the commandant.

136

The English officers gave us some rations and cigarettes and, after a day or so, we again boarded a train with the same guards and were taken to a camp in Northeast Germany. Here I saw the destruction that had resulted from the bombings — sewers were gone, the railroad station and all surrounding buildings were in rubble and the citizens were quite eager to lynch us and probably would have done so except for our guards.

The camp had separate sections for Americans and English prisoners. My stay at this camp was rather uneventful. I remained there until about late July or early August. Then, because of Russians approaching, the camp was evacuated. We were taken, in boxcars, handcuffed by pairs, to a seaport in or near Stettin. There, our handcuffs were removed, and we were loaded in the hole of a ship. There were so many of us that there was no room to lie down. Water, for food and personal hygiene, was provided by pails lowered by ropes. We always wondered whether the same pails were used.

When we disembarked from the ship, after a two to three-day voyage, our trousers were taken from us and we were again handcuffed in pairs and loaded on boxcars. These cars had a wooden log barrier that divided the car in half: one half housed guards, the other prisoners. These guards were extremely young — seemed to be in their teens.

After about two days on the train, we were unloaded. Still handcuffed, we were required to line up in columns of four. After a wait of several hours, more German guards arrived. They had motorcycles, bicycles, etc. We were told to move out at quick double time. As we ran, the guards urged us on by prodding us with bayonets. Because we were handcuffed, we had to help our partners, since if one fell the other fell. We were given to understand that if you fell you would be killed. This was made even more unnerving by the fact that we did not know how far we had to go. We ran through a couple of small towns where the population lined the streets, including many children. As we ran, they threw stones at us. The guards did nothing to deter these people so they inflicted considerable damage to the prisoners. I suffered a number of bruises and cuts. Some prisoners, I have no idea how many, died on this transfer which the Red Cross later characterized as a rather arduous journey.

When we finally arrived at the camp (about ten miles from the depot where we were unloaded), we were housed in large tents for several weeks and later moved to barracks. For the first seven months or so of my imprisonment, the rations, while not tasty, were sufficient. They consisted of an eighth of a loaf of brown bread and a cup of ersatz coffee every morning and a bowl of rutabaga soup every evening. In addition, during this period, I received three Red Cross cartons of food to supplement the rations provided by the Germans.

Because of the Russians advancing, the Germans had to evacuate the camp just before Christmas 1944. This move was made on foot. Our rations were scarce, sometimes only bread and soup every couple of days. A Red Cross van met us several times and served hot soup.

137

We walked about 20-25 miles a day. At night we were quartered in barns if such were available; if not, we slept in the fields. I am not trying to make this sound like Washington's winter at Valley Forge, but it was cold and our footwear was worn. Some prisoners died on this walk which lasted, for me, until early March of 1945, when, because of frost bite, my feet became so swollen that I couldn't walk. This was a common occurrence.

I was left with a few guards and about twenty other Americans in a barn. We were there for about a week and then taken by train to a POW camp in Northwest Germany. There we were reunited with the prisoners who had been hiking with us. This camp housed many Russians. After several days we were ordered to move out again, but my feet were still badly swollen, so I was left behind with about eight Americans and ten English prisoners and several hundred Russians.

On April 18, 1945, I awoke about five a.m. to find the camp deserted by the Germans and an hour or so later tanks of the English Eighth Army arrived. They took the American and English POWs with them and left a group to handle the Russians at the camp. We spent about two days with the English tank group and then to an American hospital in Oxford, England. I remained there about ten days. When I was captured, I weighed about 165-170 pounds. I weighed in about 110 pounds at the hospital.[9]

In mid-May I returned to the USA aboard the Queen Mary. After an overnight stay at Fort Dix, N. J., I was given an extended furlough. I remained on furlough until my discharge from the service in October 1945.

---

[9] In WWII and Korea, if captured, you were to state, "Name, Rank, and Serial #." After Korea and the loss of so many POWs and brainwashing, this rule was supplemented by a new "Code of Conduct" which did not put such a burden on captives and the guilt if they "caved in." Respect and consideration for fellow countrymen was a part of the code, with preservation of honor, but giving aid to the enemy was never condoned.

AL KUCH'S STORY

Flying tail-end Charlie, the plane piloted by Lt. Edward Adams was the first one in the 414th squadron to be shot down on the Udine Mission. Lt. Richard Munsen was the pilot on the second plane to go down. After parachuting into Yugoslavia, many of the men from both planes were found by the Partisans and walked out together.

A regular member of Adams' crew, Sgt. Al Kuch was flying his 45th mission on March 18. Kuch, a tail gunner, had almost reached the magic fifty missions necessary to request stateside duty. Six of the men flying with Adams were not part of his regular crew. They were either members of new crews who had just arrived from the States, or like Bailey Gordon, had flown only a few missions. When Gordon found Kuch in the mountains after bailing out, it is not surprising that they did not recognize one another.

When attacked by German fighters, Al Kuch had been critically injured. He was forced to stay with the Partisans until well enough to travel. In February 1992, Al wrote his story.

We were flying tail-end Charlie when we came under attack. They were coming in on our tail, and we were also being attacked from the front. I had been hit several times before the order came to bail out.

I managed to get my chest pack on. By lifting my right arm with my left, I got hold of the ring. I kept my left hand on my right arm, hoping I could pull the ring hard enough so the chute would open. I really don't know how the chute opened because when I came to, I was floating down.

I landed on a steep side hill, head down. I had one heck of a time getting out of the harness. I found that my 45 was gone. I had picked up an old hip holster that I liked better than the shoulder holster we were issued. I guess when the chute opened the jerk caused the 45 to fall out. I should have kept the shoulder holster.

So there I was on the ground, hurting, and no gun. I took off the webbed belt to get at the first aid kit, and then dropped it. I couldn't get it back on. My chute was partly hanging in a tree and I decided it was best to get away from it. I couldn't move fast because a piece of shrapnel had pierced the Achilles heel in my right foot and my elbow was bleeding badly.

Finally, I saw a small group moving ahead of me. I could tell they weren't German soldiers, so I figured they must be Partisans. They took me with them for awhile. Since I could hardly walk, one of the men helped me. The leader of the group was in a hurry and they finally left me alone.

A short time later I made contact with Bailey. We found a road going down hill and hoped to find a village. When I fell down, he'd pack snow on my face and help me get going again. By the time we reached a village it was almost dusk. I had just about had it and told Bailey I couldn't go on. Bailey helped me into the village. Thanks to him I made it.

We hoped the village wasn't under enemy control. When we contacted the first family, I was hesitant to speak German because I was afraid they would think we were Germans. However, the lady was quite sympathetic, so I decided to speak German. I explained we were Americans and looking for the Partisans.

The lady's husband wasn't happy, but she got him to go and find the Partisans who lived in the village. While the husband was gone, she heated water and soaked my arm and back. Finally, I was able to get my clothes and flak suit loose. When the husband came back with the Partisans, they took us to another building where we saw a number of other Americans.

I haven't any idea the name of the first village. The men made a stretcher for me and carried me all night. Before leaving, one of the Americans had morphine in his emergency kit and gave me a shot. I don't remember much of the first night, but I do recall it seemed like I was on "cloud nine." It must have been the morphine shot.

The next morning, we stopped at a village called Globice. This was the place where Bailey left me. Three of us were left there: a bombardier with a badly wounded foot and another airman.

The three of us stayed in Globice several days. A nurse did what she could, but with no medicine she couldn't help us much. The people were wonderful and did all they could. We had soup and brown bread to eat. The brown bread tasted so good. A couple of times we were moved out of the village when German patrols searched the homes. Once they had no warning and they hid me under heavy planks in a barn. The planks were covered with hay.

By this time gangrene had set in my arm and it was swollen to twice its normal size from hand to shoulder. I was lucky it wasn't gas forming gangrene. Later I watched and heard a young boy about 15 years old die of gas forming gangrene. That was something I never want to see or hear again.

About five days later, we were moved to a Partisan Field Hospital unit where an Italian doctor was in charge. As far as I'm concerned, this Italian doctor saved my life. He gave me a shot of morphine. I held my right hand with my left as he cut away the gangrenous flesh from my right elbow. He picked out a handful of pieces from an exploded 20mm projectile and put sulfa on the wound. Later when the wound was healing the doctor put my arm in a cast. (When I returned to the U.S. Hospital in Bari, the doctors operated again and took out the other half of the 20mm projectiles.)

The hospital unit moved many times; sometimes we were in Slovenia, other times in Croatia. But we were always in the mountains, usually where there was an old building or two that could house patients. Everything was primitive. To me the doctors and nurses performed miracles with the little they had. I think some of the medical supplies were dropped by the Allies. I know that some supplies were obtained by derailing German supply trains.

Shortly after I arrived at the Hospital Unit, scouts brought in a wounded American named Bill Abrie. He had been a waist gunner on our plane. I hadn't known him because he had just arrived from the States and was flying his first mission. (Only four of our regular crew flew on the mission to Udine: Pilot, Navigator, Radio Operator and Tail Gunner.)

Bill had been hit in the head with shrapnel and knocked out. When he came to, he was on the ground and in my tail section. Unbelievable as it sounds, when the plane blew up, the explosion forced him past the tail wheel and into the tail section. When hit, we were flying about 20,000 feet. Bill survived the explosion and the long ride down in the tail. Bill's feet were frozen, so eventually the Italian doctor amputated one leg below the knee and removed part of his other foot. I know that a train was derailed to get the anesthetic for the operation.

One time when we were moving from one place to another, we came upon a deer that had been killed by wolves. It was still warm, and the wolves had just started eating the carcass. As food was very scarce, especially meat, I wanted the Partisans to take the carcass into camp. Nobody would touch it. My arm was in a cast, so I couldn't carry it. However, I stuck my hand into the opening made by the wolves and tore out the liver. I had a hard time talking the cook into cooking the liver. When she did, only the Italian Doctor, one of the nurses and I ate it. I tried to find out why no one would take the deer into camp and why they refused to eat the liver. I still don't know why.

After I had been with the Partisans for some time, the unit was split into two groups. The walking wounded went with a Yugoslav doctor, and the Italian doctor stayed with those who couldn't walk. By this time I could walk so I went with the Yugoslav doctor. I was with this group when the cast was removed from my arm. The Doc had me carrying a sack with rocks, trying to straighten out my arm. Finally, my elbow became so sore I couldn't stand to have a shirt sleeve against it. I refused to carry the rocks any longer. I told the Doc I knew the difference between sore muscles and sore bones. The Doc and I went round and round over this. As it turned out I was right. A half a 20 mm projectile, that wasn't removed in the operation, was grinding away in my elbow.

When I left the group I went through Ljubljana, capital of Slovenia. Later we traveled through Zagreb, capital of Croatia. A Partisan soldier took me one day's journey, then another for the next day's journey, and so on. When we arrived at Tito's headquarters, I had the first good meal since I was shot down. I also had a hot bath and slept in a bed with sheets. I thought I was in heaven. They asked me if I would like to stay a few days and rest. I thought the place was great, so I said, "Yes."

141

The next day I was moved to another unit about 30 kilometers away. Here the same old stuff was served, greasy polenta and watery soup. At night I slept on planks. I made a nuisance of myself, telling them I wanted to leave. After five days they got tired of my pestering and allowed me to go. Again, a Partisan accompanied me for each day's journey.

My destination was an Allied Mission managed by the British. I was glad to be given new clothes for mine were worn out. I was outfitted in a British uniform including the shoes. The group at the Mission included French, British, Canadian, and Americans. All the Americans were officers except for me. The British and Canadians were enlisted men and among the French there was one captain. The ranking American was a first lieutenant.

The French spoke no English and the Americans didn't know French, so I spoke to the French Captain in German. I had no desire to have the French Captain leading us, so I goofed just a little when I introduced our officer as Obestleutnant (Lt. Col.) instead of Oberleutnant (First Lieutenant). Since our officers had no insignia to identify their rank and no one else spoke German, our American First Lieutenant became "boss man."

We worked our way to the area where we would be flown out. We slept in an orchard close to the landing strip. A German plane flew over and around the area almost every day. One day a Partisan got anxious and fired at the plane. The pilot dropped a few bombs. One bomb exploded not far from where I was hiding. It was so close I could have reached out and picked up a piece of shrapnel without moving. A group of wounded Partisan soldiers were waiting with us to be taken to a U.S. hospital in Italy. A C-47 came in one night and we were flown back to Bari. I had been in Yugoslavia for six months.

One of the things I dreamed about in Yugoslavia was the meal I would have when I got back to Italy. We arrived at night and the cooks had made platters of sandwiches. My stomach must have shrunk. Hungry as I was I could barely down a half sandwich. I had weighed 150 pounds when we left on the mission. When I weighed in at the hospital in Bari, I was down to 117 pounds.

I was luckier than most airmen because I could speak German and some Italian. Most of the Yugoslavs spoke either German or Italian. I even picked up a little Croatian.

When I was hospitalized in Bari the doctor operated on my arm and removed the remainder of the 20 mm projectile. I was sent back to the States on a Hospital Ship and checked in at General Holloran Hospital on Staten Island. From there I flew to El Toro Army Air Base in California. I was home for Thanksgiving in '44 and discharged with a disability in March 1945.

APPENDIX

The following excerpts are from the book, *Allied Airmen and Prisoners of War rescued by the Slovene Partisans*, published in 1946.

POBEDA
British Monthly for Yugoslavia
February 12, 1945.

MAJOR GENERAL TWINING

EXPRESSES HIS THANKS TO YUGOSLAVIA

The High Command of the AAF
February 7, 1945 (UNN)

Major General Natan F. Twining, Commander-in-chief of the 15th Air Force recently addressed the following message to the people of Yugoslavia:

"Fourteen months ago, the American Air Force started flights across Yugoslavia and many American airmen made a forced landing or bailed out into your countries.

Today instead of being German prisoners of war, they are free fighters, owing to the friendly attitude and bravery of men and women of Yugoslavia.

Disregarding your own lives and the security of your families, you saved hundreds of lives of our airmen giving them food, medical aid and shelter. You walked for miles over difficult terrain, across rivers mountains, through rain and mud, but you always brought our airmen to a safe place.

As the Commander-in-chief of the 15th AAF and in the name of the fathers and mothers of my airmen I am expressing the gratefulness of America for your valiant deeds. Our deepest thanks go also to all those who burned our dead and sent me their personal belongings.

Your bravery, patriots, who have acted under serious dangers regardless of your own security, has won the hearts of our airmen for you and has created respect for yourselves and your country."

The importance of the Slovene territory in the scheme of the Allied military operations is also confirmed by the figures on the rescued Allied airmen shot down over our territory as well as by those of the liberated Allied prisoners of war and deportees from Allied countries. These data are a living witness to the fact that our Partisan units and the detachments of the Liberation Army were in control of the whole of the Slovene territory, their activity extending even beyond it into the Austrian Styria, the northern Carinthia, and the Friuli-hind.

The Slovene people not only resisted the subjugation by the occupying forces whoever they were and however reckless, violent and bloody their rule was, but the force of the nation-wide resistance was such as to assemble all those whom the enemy thought to have made unharmful in different camps on the northern border of our territory. Numerous Allied airmen who had been shot down did not come into the hands of the enemy and hat not to be written off from the fighting ranks of the Allies.

From all places, even those remotest, lying on the farthest border of Slovenia like Graz, Spittal and Udine, safe roads led to the liberated Slovene territory. In the lapse of time from the beginning of 1944 till the complete liberation, more than 800 Allied soldiers were received here by the HQ of Slovenia and conveyed to their military units. This figure comprises only those who passed over the free Slovene territory leaving out those who remained with our Partisans fighting in our Partisan detachments.

The HQ of Slovenia were setting down three lists: the first comprising the saved American airmen, the second recording the liberated British prisoners of war and saved British airmen and the third concerning the liberated prisoners of war and deportees from France and elsewhere.

These data reveal that the Allies had a reliable basis on our territory. Due to the Partisans our territory was far from being of that service to the enemy as it had been intended to be in 1941. On the contrary: the nation-wide active resistance which embraced the whole of the Slovene territory and even draw into its ranks the near-by lying neighboring countries, placed the Slovene people together with like other Yugoslav peoples as an equal amidst the Allies that did for the common cause all it could do. There is a tendency towards overlooking this fact and the above figures are intended to draw attention to the contribution of the Partisans who had often paid for the safety of their Allied fellows in the fight against fascism with their own blood and life.

"As Senior Anglo-American Liaison officer to Headquarters Slovenia I take this opportunity to thank the National Army of Liberation and the Partisan Detachments of Slovenia and the Slovene people who support the Partisan movement under the leadership of Marshal Tito, for their considerate attention. their kind treatment, and their faithfulness to the Allied cause in the transporting, feeding, housing and the nursing, of wounded American fliers, who have been shot down front the air, by German aggressor. I realize and fully appreciate the sacrifices that are made by you to give our American fliers the kind attention they have received.

I have heard false rumors originating by German propaganda that American fliers have been disfigured and mistreated by Partisan. Slovenes. This is not true. I have talked with every American flier that has touched Slovene soil during my time of office here and each man informed me that he received only the kindest treatment and the best care from Partisan Slovenes.

The fliers think that you are wonderful people and they are very proud to be here with you during your struggle for freedom. I assure you that every Allied airplane that you see flying overhead is aware of your noble fight for freedom against the German invader and that each man sincerely hopes that if he is unfortunate enough to be shot down, that he will come into Partisan hands."

Captain J. Goodwin, head of the Anglo-American
Military Mission to Headquarters of the National Army
of Liberation. and the Partisan Detachments

July, 1944.

In 1946, The Research Institute of Ljubljana published General Twining's tribute and the names and serial numbers of hundreds of U.S. Airmen found and protected by Partisans in Slovenia. Dates the men parachuted into Northern Yugoslavia and dates they left Metlika, Slovenia are indicated. The men continued to walk through Croatia and were flown out of Bosnia the night of May 1st and 2nd.

14.   1. American Airmen

**Fortress B 17, 97 B.G. shot down near Rijeka (Fiume)
March 18, 1944, left April 9, 1944:**

55. *Richard S. Munsen. 1st lt. 0803850.*

56. *Leo B. Gordon. 2nd lt, 0666928.*

57. *Irvin E. Williamson, 2nd lt. 0591427.*

58. *Robert C. Howard, 2nd lt. 0676280.*

Fortress B 17, shot down over The Littoral, left April 9, 1944:

59. William A. Seward, 2nd lt. 0700776.

60. Samuel H. Schnear. s/sgt. 6908510.

61. Harley H. Spoon, s/sgt. 18031564.

62. Vern K. Curry. sgt. 17070043.

63. Cletus N. Reiss, sgt. 36442273.

64. Cecil R. Sullivant,. sgt. 14158579.

65. Robert Y. Brown, sgt. 35096906.

**Fortress B 17, 97 B.G. shot down near Rijeka (Fiume)
March 18, 1944, left April 9, 1944:**

66. Adam J. Pyzyna, 2nd lt. 0682590.

67. Edward J. Adams. 1st lt. 0797286.

68. Edward D. Doran, 2nd lt. 0736691.

**Fortress B 17, 2nd B.G. 96 B. SQ. shot down near Celovec
(Klagenfurt) March 19, 1944, left April 16, 1944:**

69. Thomas W. Farbes, sgt. 34172292. Gastonia, North Carolina.

70. Ascension Gonzalez, s/sgt. 18163090, Atlanta St., Tulsa, Oklahoma.

71. Russell W. Phillips, t/sgt. 15048978, 631 E. Chestnut St., Jeffersonville, Indiana.

**Fortress 13 17 shot down near Rijeka (Fiume) March 18, 1944. left
April 16, 1944:**

72. Thomas Howard, lt. 01385562.

**Fortress B 17. 463 B. G. 774 B. SQ. shot down over Styria, left
June 2. 1944:**

David Wellman, Lt. Col, retired USAF, B-52 pilot in Viet Nam, made the following comments after reading Bail Out over the Balkans.

"The fact that Dick survived 23 missions was a near miracle. The airmen who achieved the 30 mission milestone survived a 71% chance of being killed. More Army Air Force personnel died in WWII than marines. Many of the airmen died in accidents. Over 6000 B-17s were destroyed, 4700 of those in combat. 12,731 B-17s were built. Production reached a high of 16 per day in Seattle!

The B-17 was an amazing airplane. The Flying Fortress was well named since it could withstand extensive battle damage and return to base. The courage and guts of the crewmen were obviously important.

One reason for the airplane's resilience was that all systems were electric. There were no hydraulics except the landing gear struts. The belly/ball turret was turned by a shaft suspended from the top of the fuselage.

Most bomb loads were 2000 pounds on long missions. Shorter missions had up to 6000 pounds of bombs. A fully loaded B-17 weighed 61,000 pounds. In comparison, a fully loaded F-4 Phantom fighter-bomber in Viet Nam also weighed 61,000 pounds."

BIBLIOGRAPHY

MANUSCRIPT SOURCES

Unpublished accounts by downed airmen: Bob Brown, Bailey Gordon.

Letters from downed airmen: Vern Curry, Cletus Reiss, Paul Marion, Elbert Kuch, Edward Adams, Edward Doran, Joe Maloney.

Escape Statements of Richard Munsen, Cletus Reiss, Vern Curry, Irvin Williamson Courtesy of: Office of Air Force History, Reference Services Branch
Department of Air Force, Bolling Air Force Base, Washington, D. C.

97th Bombardment Group and 414th Bombardment Squadron Summaries of Missions from January 1944 through March 1944 Courtesy of: Headquarters, USAF Historical Research Center, Maxwell Air Force Base, Montgomery, Alabama.

INTERVIEWS

Ivo Matusic: former Partisan from Matulji Croatia

Crewmen: Robert Brown, Vern Curry, Cletus Reiss, Irvin Williamson, Paul Marion and Bailey Gordon

BOOKS

Allied Airmen and Prisoners of War rescued by the Slovene Partisans
    Compiled after the records of the Headquarter of Slovenia
    Published by the Research Institute, Ljubljana, 1946

Auty, Phyllis. Tito; A Biography. New York: McGraw-Hill, 1970

Bailey, Ronald H. and the editors of Time-Life Books. *Partisans and Guerrillas.* Alexandria: Time-Life Books, 1978

Cubbins, William R. *The War of the Cottontails.* Algonquin Books of Chapel Hill 1989

Davidson, Basil. *Partisan Pictures.* Bedford: Bedford Books Ltd., 1946

Deakin, F. W. D. *The Embattled Mountain.* London: Oxford University Press, 1971

Djilas, Milovan. *Wartime.* NewYork: Harcourt Brace Jovanovick, 1977

Jablonski, Edward. *Airwar: Volume IV Wings of Fire.* Garden City, New York: Doubleday and Co. Inc., 1972

Jones, Major William. *Twelve Months with Tito's Partisans.* Bedford: Bedford Books Ltd., 1946

MacLean, Fitzroy. *Eastern Approaches.* London: Jonathan Cape, 1949

Rogers, Lindsay. *Guerilla Surgeon.* London: Collins, 1957

Rust, Kenn C. *Fifteenth Air Force Story in World War II.* Temple City, CA: Historical Aviation Album, 1976

Selhaus, Edi. *Evasion and Repatriation.* Sunflower University Press, 1993

Singleton, Fred. *A Short History of the Yugoslav Peoples.* Cambridge University Press, 1985

GLOSSARY

Croatian Words and Phrases

Avioni	planes
Gospodja	prefix for a married woman
Hvala	"Thank You"
Kola	a small wooden wagon with wooden wheels
Kommandant Mesta	leader of a Communist district
Nasi	ours
Nimski	Germans
Odmor	stop
Pokret	move immediately
Polenta	porridge made from ground corn
Polje	a flat field enclosed by hills
Rakija	plum brandy, a common beverage
Samo cez ta breg	just over the next hill
Slaboda Narovu	freedom to the people
SmrtFasizmi	death to Fascism
Tishina	quiet
Zdravo	hello or health to you
Zivio	long live

EPILOGUE

A Former Pilot Returns to Croatia

A letter to the mayor of a small mountain town in Croatia — a reply — an Air Force Escape and Evasion Society (AFEES) invitation — meeting a former Partisan in St. Louis. A unique series of events led to our visit to Croatia in September 1994.

While writing *Bail Out over the Balkans* I sent letters to mayors of several towns who had protected me and my crew while we were evadees in Yugoslavia. After the mayor of Delnice received my letter he contacted Ivo Matusic, former Partisan who was interested in finding American pilots who had parachuted into Yugoslavia.

When Ivo received an invitation to attend the AFEES meeting in St. Louis in 1993, he wrote me, hoping we could meet. I attended that convention and at long last was able to say, "Thank You," to one of the Partisans who had helped me escape capture by the Germans.

Following the meeting Ivo visited our home in Story City. I spoke no Croatian, and he spoke no English. But we shared memories of risks and hardships and forged a strong bond of friendship. Ivo invited me to visit the country where I had walked fifty years before.

On September 7, 1994, Ivo greeted my wife and me at the airport in Ljubljana, Slovenia. He was wearing his AFEES pin and a white bill cap with the U.S. flag stitched on the front. After tossing our baggage into the back of his Volkswagen, we headed for Ivo's home in Croatia — about an hour's drive.

Ivo and his wife, Milka, live in Matulji, eight miles northwest of the large seaport city, Rijeka. From the Matusic veranda we could see the Adriatic Sea. Mountains were directly behind us. As we ate our evening meal, I was only four or five miles from the area where I had parachuted fifty years before.

After dinner a neighbor arrived to translate for us. He told us about the exhibition which we had seen advertised on the large, colorful posters by the side of the road. Later we heard more details from Yanko, Ivo's teenage son who spoke English fluently.

Saturday was warm and clear. At noon Ivo suggested we go outside. In a short time, we saw an airplane and thousands of leaflets sailing down.

Yanko ran to find one. Reading it, we discovered this was another of Ivo's promotions to announce my arrival for the opening of the exhibition, "They Have Been Flying Over the Sky of Istra." I had been told to prepare a short speech for the dedication in Kastav on Saturday night, but no one had mentioned that the festivities were arranged to coincide with our visit.

Kastav is a quaint medieval town overlooking the Adriatic. Narrow streets are bordered by gray stone buildings, some three stories high. People live above their shops which open onto the street. The lofty church steeple towered over the town and countryside, a symbol of protection.

We walked on uneven cobblestones to reach the city hall where invited guests gathered: two representatives from the U.S. Embassy in Zagreb, Commander of the Croatian Air Force and his adjutant, the district's legislative representative, town and area officials. Following the greetings, Mayor Cuculic presented me with a painting by a local artist.

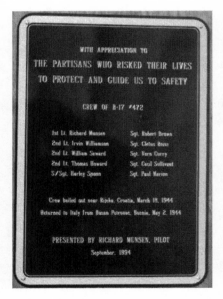

In response I gave her a plaque from my crew, expressing our appreciation to the Partisans who guided us to safety. In order that the present generation may know about the sacrifices made by those Partisans, I gave the mayor a copy of *Bail Out Over the Balkans*.

154

Guests and officials walked across the street to see the exhibition. Adopting the AFEES' motto, "We Will Never Forget," the exhibit contained pictures, newspaper articles and memorabilia from Allied airmen who had parachuted into Istra (northwestern Croatia). About 250 people crowded into the room and adjoining hallway to hear speeches given by Mayor Cuculic and Ivo. My brief remarks were translated into Croatian by an interpreter.

Ivo presenting the display of Dick and his crew

When we returned to Matulji, I recalled that Ivo had requested I write a longer speech for Sunday's celebration. I wondered how tomorrow's festivities could top the emotional impact of this night.

On Sunday morning, Ivo drove beyond Kastav, following the winding, gravel road that led to the little village of Kosi. By ten in the morning, three hundred people had assembled in the town square. A 26-piece band played as guests and dignitaries gathered in front of a small rose garden.

Among the crowd I noticed a TV camera man from Rijeka recording the band and speeches given by Ivo, President (mayor) Detan and Dr. Blatnic, former Partisan physician. A community chorus, dressed in their formal attire, sang a

Croatian folk song and Auld Lang Syne. Again, there were gifts — hand-painted ceramic pitchers for Ivo and me, red roses for Kay and Mayor Cuculic.

300 people attended the ceremonies in Kosi in September 1994

After my speech, President Detan motioned to me and an elderly woman from the village to remove the red, white and blue banner in front of the rose garden. Unveiled was a 2' by 3' black granite marker with the inscription:

"Memories of 18th March, 1944. American Pilot Richard Munsen and his crew flying in a B-17 crashed in the woods of Luziria, Kosi. September 11, 1994."

To the left of the inscription is the parachute emblem and the AFEES motto:

"We Will Never Forget."

Dick and Kay by the granite marker dedicated to his service

The band played the Star-Spangled Banner. It was a somber and emotional moment. I recalled the generosity and sacrifices made by the people of Kosi so many years ago.

With a lump in my throat I thanked the people for the honor bestowed on me. More than two hundred airmen had been protected and helped by the villagers of this community. I told them my name was representative of the other airmen as well as the many Partisans who had given their lives for the cause of freedom.

We walked by single story homes with red tile roofs and small yards where grapes were ready for harvest.

157

We came to the house with the cellar room where three of my crew and I had huddled together while German soldiers tramped above, searching for us. I was overcome with memories and gratitude for these generous people.

Going outside I looked to the east. There I saw the range of mountains where we had walked in rain and snow to evade the Germans. Beyond the horizon were the mountain villages that had offered us shelter and safety.

A table had been set up outside the house with smoked pork, bread, wine and sweets for the honored guests and visitors. There were toasts with rakija, a home-brewed plum brandy so popular in Croatia.

With the help of my interpreter I visited with former Partisans and village women who had housed and fed us fifty years before. Each one thanked me for coming to their aid when Yugoslavia was occupied by the Germans. They gave us gifts — a crocheted collar for my wife — a miniature wooden wine cask used by the Partisans for me. Although there has been no fighting in northern Croatia during this current war, the people are suffering economically. One woman said this had been the happiest day for her in four years.

I was the first airmen to return to Kosi. There were scores of mountain villages north of the Adriatic and when we parachuted none of us knew our exact location. We found the town because Bob Brown, my waist gunner, wrote the names of Kosi and Kastav in an address book he kept as a diary.

Dick with representatives of the Croation Air Force

Another town found in Bob's book was Gerovo, inland from Kosi. After the celebrations, Ivo drove us to this little mountain village, following the same route we had walked fifty years ago. The sight of the countryside gripped me.

Tree-covered mountains extended as far as the eye could see. Suddenly I was back, walking in those mountains on snow-covered trails, following our guides — just over the next hill. The feeling of hunger, the odor of unwashed clothes and bodies, and the eternal weariness of those days swept over me.

159

And now, one of the men who had guided my crew through these mountains was at the wheel of the car, skillfully managing the switchbacks in the winding road. There had been many changes since 1944, but the mountains — range after range— remained the same.

We had been invited to stay with Darinka Kovac, the English teacher with whom Kay had been corresponding. Darinka, her husband and daughter, Eva, lived in a tiny apartment at one end of the school. As we drove into the yard, we were greeted by Darinka, her parents, Drago and Rozika, and Francesca Turk, daughter of the interpreter.

Drago offered us a small glass of rakija. After several toasts we sat down to a table laden with food: pressed meat, sliced tomatoes, potato salad, pickles, a variety of Croatian pastries and tender cream puffs. After the meal, Drago pulled a mouth organ out of his pocket and began to play lively folk tunes. Francesca's eyes lit up and she swayed back and forth in time with the music. Drago put down his mouth organ and started dancing with Francesca.

Fifty years ago, dancing was a popular entertainment for the villagers. Now they were doing the same. The economy is depressed, but the spirit of the people cannot be put down.

The outpouring of love was overwhelming. Darinka and her husband gave up their bed for us. Drago got up at dawn to catch rainbow trout for our dinner. He made wooden paddles for stirring polenta to take back to my crew. He drove in heavy rain to show us the Kupa River and the little village of Turki.

I returned to Croatia to thank the people who risked their lives to save me and my crew from capture by the enemy. They responded by presenting us with gifts, treating us like royal guests, and cutting my name in stone on a marker in the Kosi town square.

It was a humbling experience. In my heart, **I will never forget.**

Made in the USA
Columbia, SC
26 October 2024

44716929R00117